NEW YORK

SCIENCE

A CLOSER LOOK

Macmillan McGraw-Hill

Program Authors

Dr. Jay K. Hackett
Professor Emeritus of Earth Sciences
University of Northern Colorado
Greeley, CO

Dr. Richard H. Moyer
Professor of Science Education and
   Natural Sciences
University of Michigan–Dearborn
Dearborn, MI

Dr. JoAnne Vasquez
Elementary Science Education Consultant
NSTA Past President
Member, National Science Board
   and NASA Education Board

Mulugheta Teferi, M.A.
Principal, Gateway Middle School
Center of Math, Science, and Technology
St. Louis Public Schools
St. Louis, MO

Dinah Zike, M.Ed.
Dinah Might Adventures LP
San Antonio, TX

Kathryn LeRoy, M.S.
Executive Director
Division of Mathematics and Science Education
Miami-Dade County Public Schools, FL
Miami, FL

Dr. Dorothy J. T. Terman
Science Curriculum Development Consultant
Former K–12 Science and Mathematics Coordinator
Irvine Unified School District, CA
Irvine, CA

Dr. Gerald F. Wheeler
Executive Director
National Science Teachers Association

Bank Street College of Education
New York, NY

Contributing Authors

Dr. Sally Ride
Sally Ride Science
San Diego, CA

Lucille Villegas Barrera, M.Ed.
Elementary Science Supervisor
Houston Independent School District
Houston, TX

American Museum of Natural History
New York, NY

Contributing Writer

Ellen C. Grace, M.S.
Consultant
Albuquerque, NM

RFB&D Students with print disabilities may be eligible to obtain an accessible, audio version of the pupil edition of this
learning through listening textbook. Please call Recording for the Blind & Dyslexic at 1-800-221-4792 for complete information.

A

The McGraw·Hill Companies

Macmillan/McGraw-Hill

Send all inquiries to:
Macmillan/McGraw-Hill
8787 Orion Place
Columbus, OH 43240-4027

ISBN: 978-0-02-287563-3
MHID: 0-02-287563-8

Printed in the United States of America.

1 2 3 4 5 6 7 8 9 (027/043) 12 11 10 09 08 07

The American Museum of Natural History in New York City is one of the world's preeminent scientific, educational, and cultural institutions, with a global mission to explore and interpret human cultures and the natural world through scientific research, education, and exhibitions. Each year the Museum welcomes around four million visitors, including 500,000 schoolchildren in organized field trips. It provides professional development activities for thousands of teachers; hundreds of public programs that serve audiences ranging from preschoolers to seniors; and an array of learning and teaching resources for use in homes, schools, and community-based settings. Visit www.amnh.org for online resources.

 is a trademark of The McGraw-Hill Companies, Inc.

Be a Scientist

Scientific Method

Observe

↓

Ask a Question

↓

Make a Prediction

↓

Make a Plan

↓

Follow the Plan

↓

Record the Results

↓

Try the Plan Again

↓

Draw a Conclusion

Life Science

Earth Science

Physical Science

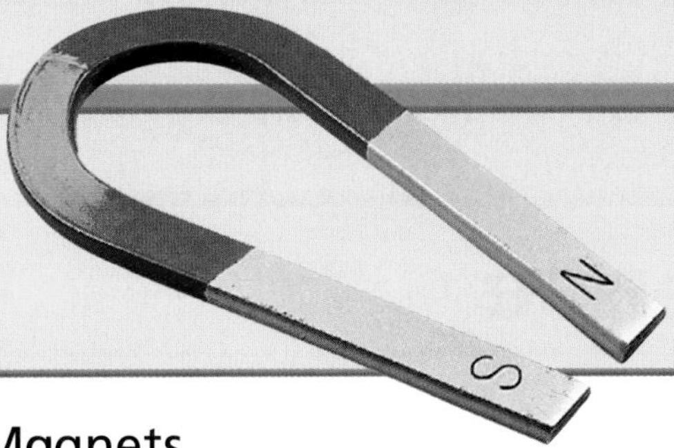

CHAPTER 8 ▬▬▬▬▬▬▬▬▬▬▬▬▬▬

Using Energy 296

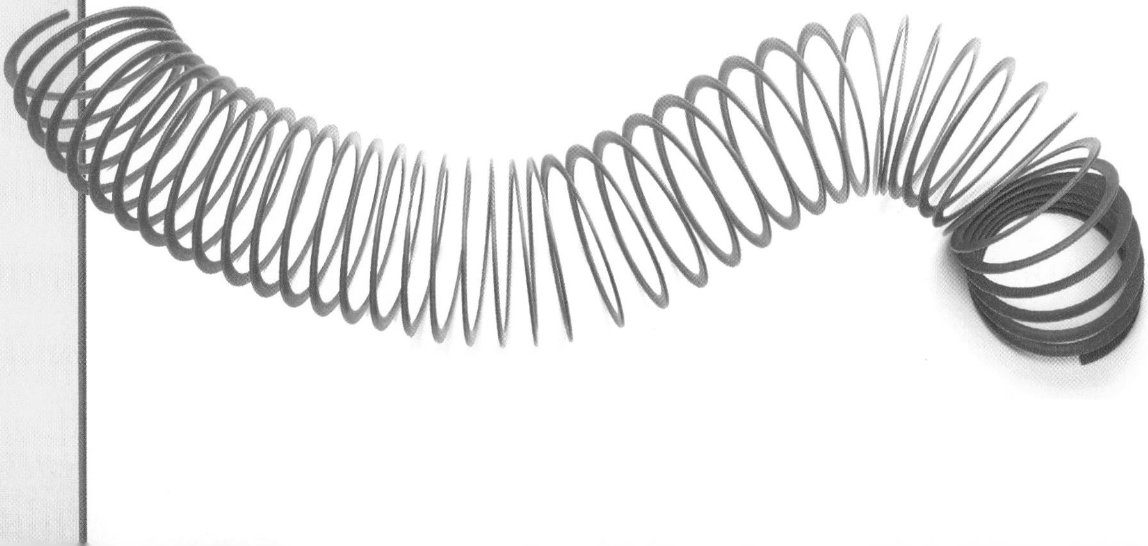

Activities and Investigations

Life Science

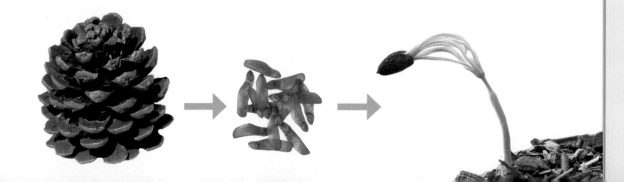

Earth Science

Activities and Investigations

Physical Science

Be a Scientist

Some tree frogs lay their eggs
on leaves floating on water.

Science Skills

Look and Wonder

Do you see the frog? How does it stay on the lily pad?

SI. The central purpose of scientific inquiry is to develop explanations of natural phenomena in a continuing, creative process.

How can a frog float on a lily pad?

You need

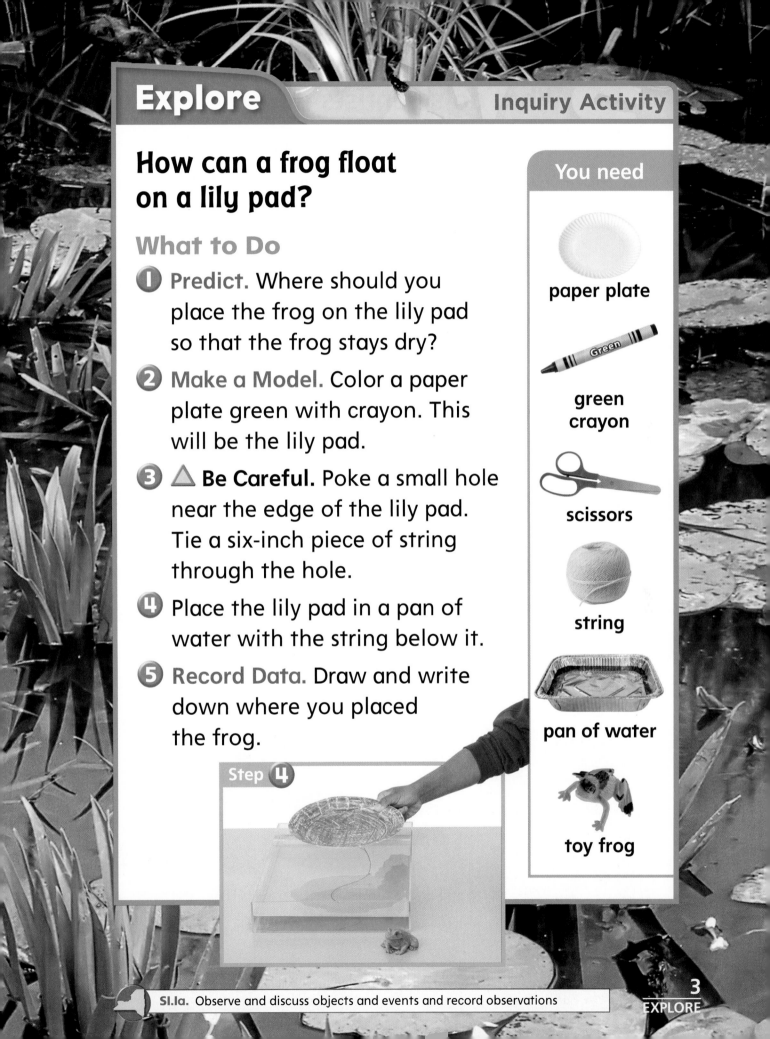

paper plate

green crayon

scissors

string

pan of water

toy frog

What to Do

1. **Predict.** Where should you place the frog on the lily pad so that the frog stays dry?

2. **Make a Model.** Color a paper plate green with crayon. This will be the lily pad.

3. ⚠️ **Be Careful.** Poke a small hole near the edge of the lily pad. Tie a six-inch piece of string through the hole.

4. Place the lily pad in a pan of water with the string below it.

5. **Record Data.** Draw and write down where you placed the frog.

Step 4

SI.Ia. Observe and discuss objects and events and record observations

What do scientists do?

Scientists use many skills when they work. You wondered about the frog on a lily pad. Just as you did, a scientist might **make a model** to help answer a question. A model shows how something in real life looks.

Scientists use other skills that you can use, too. Scientists **observe**, or look carefully. A scientist who observes a pond can find many amazing things.

Scientists observe the height, color, and shape of plants near the pond.

cattails

pond grass

water iris

Scientists **compare** things by telling how they are alike or different. Look at the two pond animals on this page. How might a scientist compare them?

Look closely. Both animals have wings. They both live near ponds. But they are different in many other ways.

Scientists find ways to **classify** things, or put them in groups. Insects and birds are different animal groups.

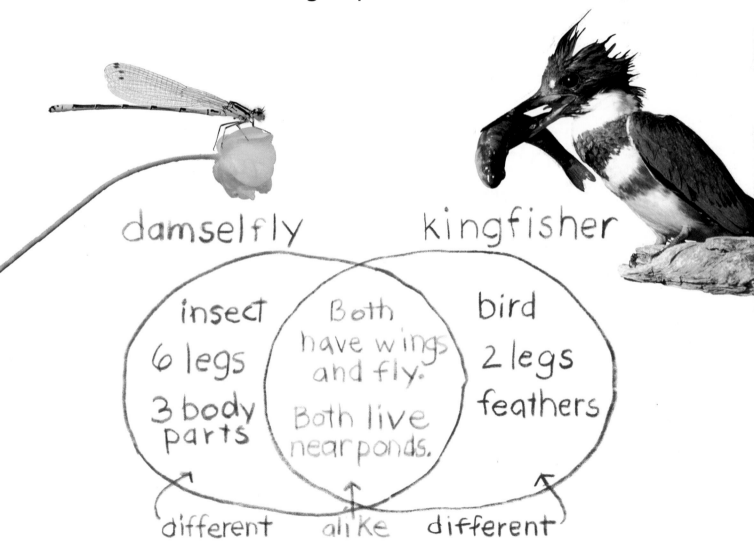

damselfly   kingfisher

insect
6 legs
3 body
parts

Both
have wings
and fly.

Both live
near ponds.

bird
2 legs
feathers

different   alike   different

How do scientists work?

Look at all the eggs a scientist found near a pond! Scientists can **measure** how large or how heavy the eggs are. When you measure, you find out how long or how heavy something is. You can also find out how hot or how cold something is.

The facts scientists find are called data. When scientists **record data**, they write down what they observe.

How long?

turtle	3 centimeters
frog	3 millimeters
duck	5 centimeters
robin	2 centimeters

After scientists collect data, they can put their data in order. **Put things in order** means to arrange things in some way. For example, you can order eggs by their size. Which egg is smallest? Which is largest?

Another skill scientists use is **infer**. When you infer, you use what you know to figure something out. Can you infer which eggs belong to the animals on this page?

frog

duck

turtle

robin

How do scientists learn new things?

Scientists learn new things by investigating. When you **investigate**, you make a plan and try it out.

Scientists start by asking a question. They predict what the answer might be. When you **predict**, you use what you know to tell what you think will happen.

Look at the pictures of the tadpole and young frog. What do you predict the young frog will look like next?

tadpole

young frog

?

?

When you **draw conclusions**, you use what you observe to explain what happens. Scientists draw conclusions. They conclude tadpoles live in the water, grow legs, and climb onto land.

Scientists communicate their ideas to other people. When you **communicate**, you write, draw, or tell your ideas.

September 17

My Frog Notes

← head
← tail

First, it was a tadpole.

legs

Then the tadpole grew legs. It still has a tail.

short legs

no tail

long legs

Now it has long back legs and no tail.

My Conclusion:

Frogs grow legs and can walk on land.

Think, Talk, and Write

1. Which skill helps scientists put things into groups?

2. Write about what new things you might want to learn if you were a scientist.

Scientific Method

Look and Wonder

This frog can swim! How else can a frog move? Scientists ask questions like this. They follow certain steps to find the answers.

S2. Beyond the use of reasoning and consensus, scientific inquiry involves the testing of proposed explanations involving the use of conventional techniques and procedures.... **S3.** The observations made while testing proposed explanations ... provide new insights into phenomena.

How does a frog move?

What to Do

1. **Observe.** Look at the pictures on this page. Think about how the frogs are moving.

2. **Record Data.** Make a list of the different ways you see the frogs moving.

3. **Draw Conclusions.** Add to your list. Write the body part the frogs use to move in each way.

4. **Communicate.** Talk with a partner about how frogs move. Make new observations if you and your partner disagree.

S3.2a. State, orally and in writing, any inferences or generalizations indicated by the data collected

How high can a frog jump?

Scientists investigate by following steps called the **Scientific Method**. Here is how one student scientist follows the Scientific Method.

Observe

Lola uses her science skills to observe the frogs in her classroom.

Ask a Question

Lola's question is:

Does a frog's size affect how far it jumps?

Make a Prediction

Lola predicts the answer is yes. She thinks Andy will jump farther because his legs are longer.

Andy   Molly

Make a Plan

Lola writes down a plan to test her idea. When she writes the plan, other people can follow it too.

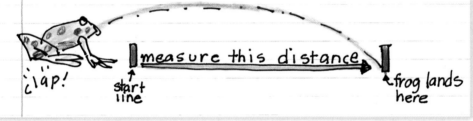

My Frog Jumping Plan

① Make a starting line on the floor.

② Place one frog behind the starting line.

   Clap to make it jump.

   Measure how far the frog jumped.

③ Repeat step ② with the other frog.

¡clap! start line measure this distance frog lands here

Follow the Plan

Lola follows her plan. She changes the plan if parts of it do not work.

What did you find out?

Record the Results

Lola makes a chart to show how far each frog jumps.

How far can each frog jump?			
frog	1st try	2nd try	3rd try
 Andy	20 cm		
 Molly	25 cm		

Try the Plan Again

Lola tests each frog three times. This helps her know if her results are correct.

Draw a Conclusion

Lola explains what her results mean.

Lola talks to her classmates about what her results mean. This can lead to new questions and new investigations.

You can follow the Scientific Method when you investigate too!

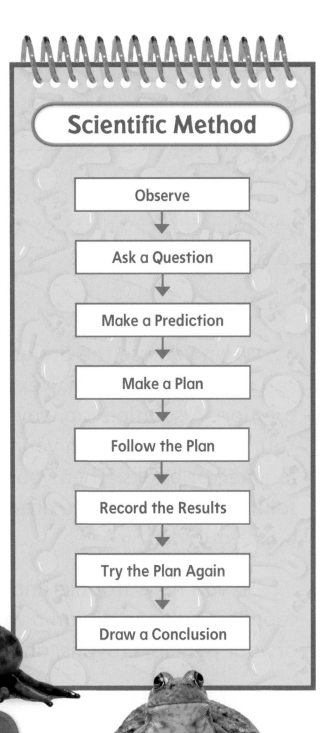

Scientific Method

Observe

↓

Ask a Question

↓

Make a Prediction

↓

Make a Plan

↓

Follow the Plan

↓

Record the Results

↓

Try the Plan Again

↓

Draw a Conclusion

Think, Talk, and Write

1. Why do you think it is important for scientists to make a plan?

2. Write about why scientists write down their plans.

Science and Technology:
The Design Process

Have you ever had a problem? How did you solve it? Scientists use the **design process** to solve problems.

▶ Learn It

When you use the design process, first you identify a problem. Next you think of a solution. A solution is a way to fix a problem. You can get ideas from your friends, a teacher, or books. Then you design your solution. To design is to draw, plan, and build your idea.

Do you have trouble finding your school supplies? You can design a way to keep track of your pencils, crayons, and other supplies.

▶ Try It

Michael designed a box to hold all of his school supplies. Michael's box had a place for his pencils, crayons, glue, and eraser.

Design a way to store your school supplies. Make a sketch of your idea. Share your idea with your teacher. Gather the materials that you need for your design. Build your invention and test your design.

1. How does your design compare to Michael's?

2. Does your design solve your problem?

3. Write about it. How could you change your design to make it better?

 TI.4. Plan and build, under supervision, a model of the solution, using familiar materials, processes, and hand tools. **TI.5c.** Analyze results and suggest how to improve the solution or model, using oral, graphic, or written formats.

When you see △ Be Careful, follow the safety rules.

Tell your teacher about accidents
and spills right away.

Be careful with sharp
objects and glass.

Wear goggles when
you are told to.

Wash your hands
after each activity.

Keep your workplace neat.
Clean up when you are done.

Life Science

Woodchucks eat plants and sharpen their claws on trees.

Sugar Maples in New York

tapping a maple
tree

American Maple
Museum

Syrup Comes From Trees

How many different kinds of trees can you name? The sugar maple tree is special to New York. People use sap from sugar maples to make maple syrup.

In Croghan, New York, you can find the American Maple Museum. In the museum you will see tools that people can use to make maple syrup.

Trees Are Important

Humans and animals use trees in a lot of ways. Humans cut down trees to make paper and to build homes. Animals like squirrels and birds use trees as their homes.

 Think, Talk, and Write

Critical Thinking What can we do to use fewer trees to make the things we need?

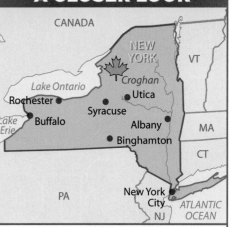

New York
A CLOSER LOOK

CANADA

NEW YORK

VT

Lake Ontario
Croghan
Rochester
Utica
Lake Erie
Syracuse
Buffalo
Albany
MA
Binghamton
CT

PA
New York City
NJ
ATLANTIC OCEAN

▶ **Main Idea**
Humans and other animals need trees for many things.

▶ **Activity**

Communicate
Make a poster to show the importance of trees.

■ Write about how trees are important.

■ Draw pictures to show how humans and other animals use trees.

LE-7.1c. Humans, as individuals or communities, change environments in ways that can be either helpful or harmful for themselves and other organisms.

Beavers Return to the Bronx River

José the Bronx
River Beaver

A Changing River

Did you know the Bronx River is home to many plants and animals? This has not always been true. Pollution once made the Bronx River dirty. Animals and plants could not use the river as a home.

A Beaver Returns

Many people have worked to clean up the Bronx River. Plants and animals that used to live here have returned. In 2007 scientists saw a beaver! This beaver is the first in the Bronx River for over 200 years! The scientists named the beaver José. Scientists hope many other beavers will return to the Bronx River.

Think, Talk, and Write

Critical Thinking Why is it important to keep the Bronx River clean?

 LE-6.If. When the environment changes, some plants and animals survive and reproduce, and others die or move to new locations.

CANADA

NEW YORK

VT

Lake Ontario

Rochester • • Utica

Lake Erie • Buffalo

Syracuse

Albany

MA

• Binghamton

CT

PA

Bronx River

New York City

NJ

ATLANTIC OCEAN

▶ **Main Idea**

Plants and animals depend on each other and their environment.

▶ **Activity**

Investigate What plants and animals live in the Bronx River?

■ Use reference materials to make a list.

■ Share your list with a classmate.

CHAPTER **1**

Plants

How do plants grow and change?

New Zealand rain forest

Key Vocabulary

flower plant part that makes seeds or fruit (page 36)

seed plant part that can grow into a new plant (page 36)

pollen sticky powder inside a flower that helps make seeds (page 36)

seedling a young plant (page 40)

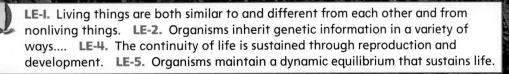

LE-1. Living things are both similar to and different from each other and from nonliving things.   **LE-2.** Organisms inherit genetic information in a variety of ways....   **LE-4.** The continuity of life is sustained through reproduction and development.   **LE-5.** Organisms maintain a dynamic equilibrium that sustains life.

What Living Things Need

farm in Pomfret, Vermont

Look and Wonder

What things in this picture are alive? How can you tell?

 LE-4.2 (b). Describe evidence of growth, repair, and maintenance, such as nails, hair, and bone, and the healing of cuts and bruises. **LE-5.1 (a).** Describe basic life functions of common living specimens....

What do leaves need?

What to Do

1. Put the plants in a sunny place. Choose one plant and cover its leaves with foil. Keep the soil moist in both pots.

2. **Predict.** What will happen to each plant in a week?

3. **Record Data.** Write down what you observe for a week.

4. Were your predictions correct? What do leaves need?

Explore More

5. **Predict.** What will happen if the foil is removed? Observe the plant for a week. Was your prediction correct?

You need

two potted plants

foil

Step 1

A   B

Vocabulary

minerals

oxygen

What do living things need?

Living things grow and change. Sometimes it is easy to tell when something is living. You can see animals move, breathe air, eat food, and drink water. It might be harder to tell, but plants are living things, too.

◄ A grasshopper eats a dandelion flower.

The swan makes a nest for her chicks near a pond.

You have to watch plants over time to see them change and grow. Like all living things, plants need air, water, and space to live and grow. They also need food. Plants make their own food.

✓ **What makes living things grow?**

▼ **This sunflower takes most of the summer to grow into an adult plant.**

sprout

young plant

adult plant

How do plants make food?

Plants have parts that they use to help them make food. Plants need sunlight, air, and water to make their own food. Plants also need minerals. **Minerals** are bits of rock and soil that help plants and animals grow.

Quick Lab

Observe a plant. See what parts take in water.

Plants Make Food

Leaves take in air and use sunlight to make food. ———

The stem holds up the plant. It allows water and food to travel through the plant. ———

Roots hold the plant in the soil. They also take in water and minerals. ——— Roots can store food for the plant, too.

Read a Diagram

How do the parts of the plant help it get what it needs to make food?

When plants make food they give off a gas called oxygen into the air. **Oxygen** is what humans and other animals breathe in order to live.

▼ These plants make oxygen that the boy and the dog need to live.

 What do plants need to make food?

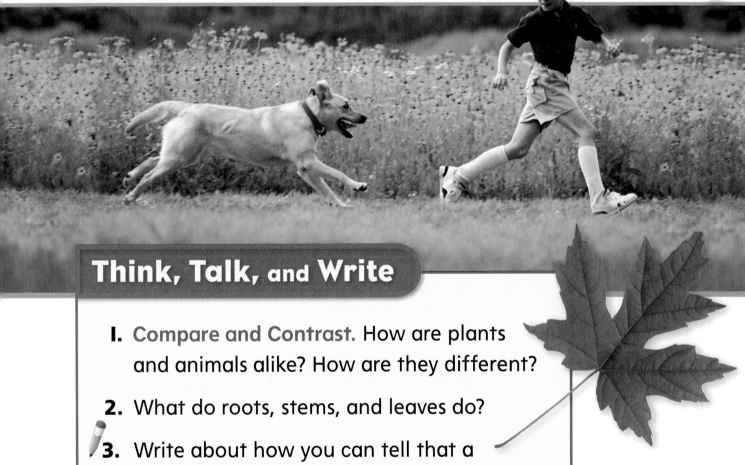

Think, Talk, and Write

1. **Compare and Contrast.** How are plants and animals alike? How are they different?

2. What do roots, stems, and leaves do?

3. Write about how you can tell that a plant is living.

Art Link

Draw how a seed grows. What direction do the roots grow? What direction do the stem and leaves grow?

 e-Review Summaries and quizzes on line at **www.macmillanmh.com**.

Focus on Skills

Inquiry Skill: Observe

To **observe**, you use your senses to learn about something. You use senses to see, hear, taste, smell, and touch.

▶ Learn It

You can use some of your senses to learn about flowers. You can make a chart to write down what you observe.

jasmine

jasmine

see	
feel	The leaves feel smooth.
hear	
smell	The flowers smell sweet.

S2.3b. Record observations accurately and concisely

► **Try It**

Find a flower to observe or look at the pictures below.

bougainvillea

yucca plant

1. What color is your flower? Which sense did you use to find out?

2. How do you think the leaves will feel to your touch?

3. Write About It. Find another flower and compare.

Plants Make New Plants

Look and Wonder

Where do you think the seeds in this plant are?

 LE-1.1 (b). Describe the characteristics of and variations between living and nonliving things. **LE-4.1 (c,d).** Describe the major stages in the life cycles of selected plants and animals.

What are the parts of a seed?

What to Do

1 **Observe.** What does the outside of a dry lima bean feel like? Use a hand lens. What do you see?

2 **Predict.** Draw what you think is inside the seed.

3 Use your fingernail to open the wet seed. Use your hand lens to observe the wet seed. Draw what you see.

4 **Communicate.** Compare your two drawings. What was different? What was the same?

Explore More

5 **Observe.** Look at other wet and dry seeds to see how they compare.

You need

dry lima bean

wet lima bean

hand lens

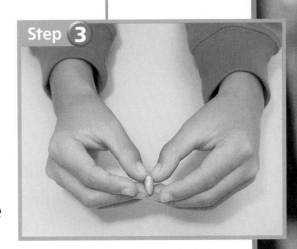

Step **3**

Where do seeds come from?

A **flower** is the part of a plant that makes seeds and fruit. A **seed** is the part of a plant that can grow into a new plant.

Part of the flower makes pollen. **Pollen** is a sticky powder inside the flower that helps make seeds.

Cantaloupe

Pollen lands on this part of the flower and helps it make seeds.

This part of the flower grows into a fruit with seeds.

Animals such as birds and bees can move pollen between flowers. Wind and water can move pollen, too.

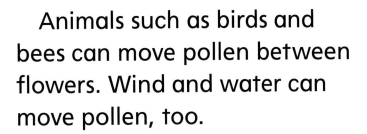

✅ **What does pollen help a plant make?**

▲ **Hummingbirds drink nectar from flowers and move pollen from plant to plant.**

▲ **The fruit protects the seeds inside.**

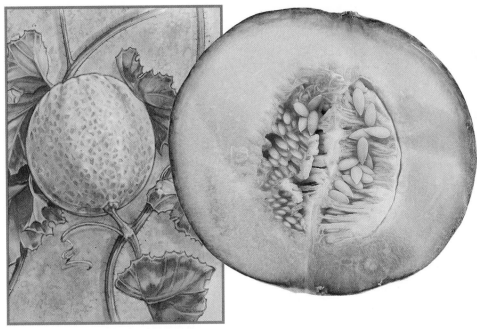

▲ **When the fruit is ripe, it can be picked.**

▲ **The seeds inside the fruit can grow into new plants.**

How do seeds look?

Most plants have seeds to make new plants. Seeds have food inside them to help the new plant grow. There are many different shapes and sizes of seeds.

Some seeds are small. Wind or water can carry them away. Other seeds stick to the fur of animals and get a ride to a new place.

Quick Lab

Observe the seeds inside an apple. Talk about how the fruit protects the seeds.

◄ There are many anise seeds inside this star-shaped pod. The shapes of the pod and the flower are alike.

▲ A marigold seed is small and thin. It does not have much food inside.

Seeds have many parts. All seeds have seed coats which protect the seed. Seed coats also help keep the seeds from drying out. Some seeds also have hard shells.

 Why do you think some seeds have shells?

▲ **Peanuts are seeds. They come from peanut plants.**

The shell of a peanut is hard and light brown.

The seed coat is thin and dark brown.

This part is a tiny plant. It will grow bigger.

These parts give food to the tiny plant so it can grow.

FACT Seeds are living things.

How do seeds grow?

A **life cycle** shows how a living thing grows, lives, makes more of its own kind, and dies. The plant life cycle begins with a seed. Seeds need a warm place, light, water, and food in order to grow.

Life Cycle of a Pine Tree

Adult pine trees make seeds in cones instead of flowers.

The pine cones fall to the ground. Some seeds get moved to other places.

A seed sprouts and becomes a **seedling**, or young plant.

The seedling grows into an adult pine tree. It grows cones so it can make new plants.

Read a Diagram

What does a pine tree have instead of flowers?

LOG ON *Science in Motion* Watch a plant grow at **www.macmillanmh.com**

Most plants follow the same life cycles as their parent plants. Different kinds of plants have different life cycles. Some plants live for just a few weeks. Other plants live for many years.

 What will a pine seed grow into?

◄ **These flowers go through their whole life cycle in just a few months.**

▲ **Redwood trees take more than two years just to make cones.**

Think, Talk, and Write

1. **Sequence.** How do flowers make new plants?

2. How would you take care of seeds to help them grow?

3. Write or draw pictures to show the steps in the life cycle of a plant.

Health Link

We eat the fruit and seeds of many plants. How many can you think of? What other plant parts do we eat?

 e-Review Summaries and quizzes online at **www.macmillanmh.com**

Main Idea and Details

Read about a plant that uses wind to move its seeds. The main idea is circled. The details are underlined.

Dandelions

Dandelions use the wind to move their seeds. Dandelion petals dry out when the flower dies. Then the seeds are ready to come off the flower. The seeds have long light tufts that can float in the air. Wind blows the seeds. They land in places where new plants can grow.

 Write About It

Write a paragraph about a flower that you observed. Make sure you have a main idea and details.

Remember

The main idea tells what a paragraph is about. Details tell more about the main idea.

 LOG ON **e-Journal** Write about it online at **www.macmillanmh.com**

S3.2a. State, orally and in writing, any inferences or generalizations indicated by the data collected

How Many Seeds?

Some fruits, like watermelons, have many seeds. Other fruits, like peaches, have just one seed.

Solve a Problem

Suppose each apple on this tree had about 5 seeds. If you picked 3 apples, about how many seeds would you have? Show how you found the answer.

Write a number sentence about fruit seeds. Show your work.

Remember
You can draw pictures to help you find the answer.

 MI.Ia. Use plus, minus, greater than, less than, equal to, multiplication, and division signs

How Plants Are Alike and Different

mangrove roots in the Philippines

Look and Wonder

Look at these plants. Which way do you think the roots are growing?

LE-2.2 (a,b). Recognize that for humans and other living things there is genetic continuity between generations. **LE-5.2(a).** Describe some survival behaviors of common living specimens.

How do roots grow?

What to Do

① Put three bean seeds on a damp paper towel. Put them in the bag and tape it to a bulletin board.

3 bean seeds

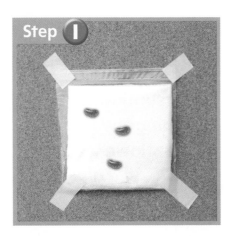

Step ①

paper towels

② **Observe.** Which part grows first? Which way did the roots grow?

③ After the roots grow, turn the bag upside down. Tape it to the board again. Make sure the paper towel stays wet.

④ **Draw Conclusions.** What happened to the roots?

Explore More

⑤ **Investigate.** What happens to the roots if left in the dark?

tape

plastic bag

hand lens

S2.3a. Use appropriate "inquiry and process skills" to collect data
S2.3b. Record observations accurately and concisely

How are plants like their parents?

You know that cats have kittens and dogs have puppies. Animals have babies that look and act like their parents. Plants do the same thing.

▼ An acorn can grow into an oak tree.

▶ A sunflower seed can grow into a sunflower.

The way plants or animals look or act is called a **trait**. Young plants will have many of the same traits as their parents. Some plants might look a little different from their parents. The plant will still have the same shape of flowers, petals, and leaves.

▲ **Long ears are a trait of basset hounds.**

✓ **What are some traits of a sunflower?**

Tulips

Read a Photo

How are these tulips alike and different?

How do plants survive in different places?

Plants change to get what they need from the place where they live. When a seed begins to grow, the roots always grow down. Plant parts may look different in different places, but their parts still help make food.

▲ This Joshua tree and other plants in very dry places have few or no leaves. These plants store water in thick stems.

▲ This banana tree and other plants in very wet places have large leaves. They help get light in the thick, dark forest.

Plants can change to stay safe, too. Some plants have ways to stay safe from animals. Other plants need to stay safe from the weather where they live. When plants change during their lives, those traits are not passed down to their offspring.

✓ Why do you think some plants have thorns?

◀ On the coast, the wind is so strong that the branches on the trees bend.

Think, Talk, and Write

1. **Classify.** Think of four ways that plants are like their parent plants.

2. What changes the way plants grow?

3. Write about the way a plant grows from a seed. How do the roots grow? Why?

Art Link

Make a crayon rubbing of two different leaves. How are they alike? How are they different?

The Power of Periwinkle

People who live in forests all over the world know about helpful plants. They use plants for food and for building homes. They also use plants to make medicine.

One helpful plant is the rosy periwinkle. It first grew in Madagascar, and later people spread it around the world. People now use the plant to treat fevers, sore throats, toothaches, and upset stomachs.

Today some forests in Madagascar are being cut down. People clear the land to grow food. Scientists want to keep these forests safe. There may be more helpful plants to study and use.

Madagascar

AMERICAN MUSEUM of NATURAL HISTORY

S3.Ia. Accurately transfer data from a science journal or notes to appropriate graphic organizer

▲ Scientists and local people use the rosy periwinkle to treat diseases.

This woman gathers rosy periwinkle plants. ▶

Talk About It

Classify. Make a list of plants you know. Classify them by how they help people.

Peach Tree

This plant is a peach tree. It is living. Its leaves use light from the Sun to make food. Its roots get water from the ground. The peaches it makes are fruit. Each peach has a seed inside.

Seeds need water and a warm place to grow. The roots grow down into the ground. The stems and leaves grow up toward the light. This peach tree will grow to look like its parent plant.

The tree grows bigger and
makes flowers. Flowers help
the plant make new plants.
Many of these flowers
will grow into peaches.

This tree is covered in peaches. People and animals eat the peaches and leave the seeds behind. The seeds can grow into new peach trees.

Vocabulary

Use each word once for items 1–5.

flower

life cycle

pollen

seed

traits

1. A _____ shows how something grows, lives, and dies.
LE-4.1 (a,b,c,d)

2. The part of the plant that makes the seed is called the _____.
LE-3.1 (b)

3. The ways that plants and animals look like their parents are called _____.
LE-2.2 (a,b)

4. Flowers need a sticky powder called _____ to make seeds.
LE-3.1 (b)

5. This is a _____. It will grow into a new plant.
LE-3.1 (b)

Answer the questions below.

6. Compare and Contrast. Look at the pictures below. What traits do these plants share?
LE-3.I (c)

7. What do seeds and seedlings need to live and grow?
LE-I.I (b); LE-3.I (b)

8. Observe. Look at the plants in the picture below. Describe them.
LE-3.I (c)

9. How do plants grow and change? LE-I; LE-2; LE-4; LE-5

Animals

The Big Idea

How do animals grow and change?

Key Vocabulary

More Vocabulary

mammal animal with hair or fur that feeds milk to its young (page 62)

amphibian, page 63

reptile, page 63

life cycle, page 70

pupa, page 72

camouflage, page 79

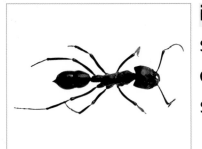

insect animal with six legs, antennae, and a hard outer shell (page 64)

larva stage in the life cycle of some animals after they hatch from an egg (page 72)

adaptation body part or way animal acts that helps it stay alive (page 78)

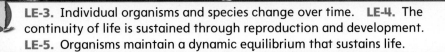

LE-3. Individual organisms and species change over time. **LE-4.** The continuity of life is sustained through reproduction and development. **LE-5.** Organisms maintain a dynamic equilibrium that sustains life.

Animal Groups

crabs and iguanas in the Galapagos Islands

Look and Wonder

There are thousands of different kinds of animals. How are these animals alike and different?

 Building Block Lesson for LE-5.Ib. An organism's external physical features can enable it to carry out life functions in its particular environment.

How can we put animals into groups?

What to Do

1. **Classify.** Look at the pictures of the animals. Put the animals into groups. How did you decide to group the animals?

2. Talk about the animal groups with a partner. What groups did your partner use?

3. **Compare.** How are your groups and your partner's groups alike? How are they different?

Explore More

4. **Classify.** Think about animals that live on land. How can you classify them?

SI.2a. Identify similarities and differences between explanations received from others or in print and personal observations or understandings

Read Together and Learn

Vocabulary

mammal

amphibian

reptile

insect

How do we group animals?

All animals need food, water, air, shelter, and space to live. They have different parts that help them get what they need to live.

Scientists classify animals into two main groups. One group has backbones. The other group does not have backbones. Here are some animals with backbones.

These lions are mammals. A mammal is an animal that has hair or fur. A female mammal makes milk for her babies. Mammals breathe through their lungs. ▼

This is a bluebird. Birds are the only animals with feathers. All birds have two wings and a beak to help them get food. They lay eggs to hatch their young. ▶

▲ Fish, such as this salmon, live in water. Their gills help them breathe. Their fins help them swim.

▶ This salamander is an amphibian. Most amphibians begin their lives in water. Their moist skin helps them live on land and in water.

This baby alligator is a reptile. It has rough, scaly skin to help protect it. ▼

 Why is a lion a mammal?

FACT ▶ Birds are not the only animals that hatch from eggs. Other animals such as alligators, butterflies, and snakes do, too!

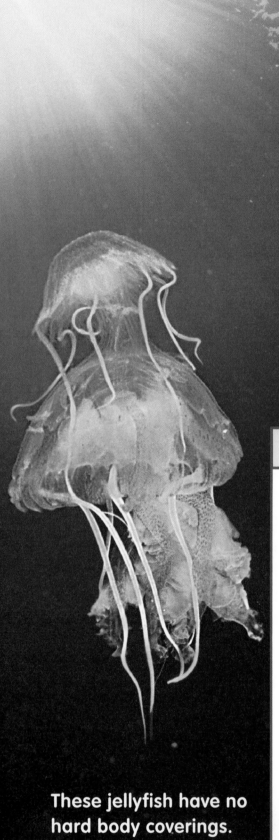

These jellyfish have no hard body coverings. They sting other animals to stay safe and get food.

What are some animals without backbones?

There are many kinds of animals that have no backbones. There are more without backbones than with backbones! Some animals without backbones have hard body coverings to help them stay safe.

An **insect** is an animal with six legs, antennae, and a hard, outer shell.

The antenna helps insects feel, taste, and smell.

The outer shell helps keep insects safe. The legs help insects climb on smooth or rough places.

Read a Diagram

How do the body parts of a beetle help it meet its needs?

> The dragonfly has a hard body covering. It uses its wings to fly away from its enemies.

Quick Lab

Make a model of an animal. Talk with a partner about how the animal meets its needs.

 How do animals without backbones stay safe?

blue crayfish

Think, Talk, and Write

1. **Classify.** How can you classify a lion and a salamander?

2. What do animals need to stay alive?

3. Choose one animal. Write about a body part from that animal. Describe how it helps the animal meet its needs.

Social Studies Link

Make a collage of other animals without backbones. Find out where they live.

LOG ON **e-Review** Summaries and quizzes online at www.macmillanmh.com

earthworm

Focus on Skills

Inquiry Skill: Classify

When you **classify**, you put things into groups to show how they are alike.

▶ Learn It

You can use a chart to classify what you learned about animals.

rabbit

sparrow

Different Animals

Mammals	Reptiles	Birds
sheep	lizard	eagle
mouse	turtle	sparrow

sheep

 S3.Ia. Accurately transfer data from a science journal or notes to appropriate graphic organizer

▶ **Try It**

Use a chart to classify these animals. Add other animals to your chart. Share your chart with a partner.

parrot

guinea pig

penguin

iguana

▶ **Try It**

1. How are mammals and birds alike? How are they different?

2. What ways did you classify the animals in your chart?

3. Write About It. How is your chart different from the chart your partner made?

snake

Animals Grow and Change

Look and Wonder

How are baby animals different from their parents?

 LE-4.1 (e). Describe the major stages in the life cycles of selected plants and animals. **LE-4.2 (a).** Describe evidence of growth, repair, and maintenance, such as nails, hair, and bone, and the healing of cuts and bruises.

How are babies and adults alike and different?

What to Do

1. What are some things that babies do?

2. What are some things adults do?

3. **Compare.** Make a Venn diagram to compare babies to adults.

Explore More

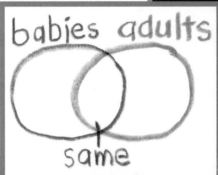

4. How are baby humans and baby tigers alike and different?

SI.3a. Clearly express a tentative explanation or description which can be tested

What is a life cycle?

Insects, birds, fish, reptiles, and amphibians lay eggs. Mammals give birth to live babies. Chickens are birds and they lay eggs. All animals have a life cycle. A **life cycle** tells how an animal starts life, grows to be an adult, has young, and dies.

Giant Panda Life Cycle

Baby pandas grow inside their mothers' bodies. They drink milk from their mothers so they can grow.

Chicken Life Cycle

Baby chickens, or chicks, break the shell to get out of an egg. They can see, walk, and feed themselves after they hatch.

Quick Lab

Communicate.
Act out a life cycle
of an animal.

✓ **What are the stages
of a life cycle?**

A baby panda grows
up to be an adult.
It may find a mate
and have a baby
of its own.

The chicks
grow up to
be adult chickens.
This is a rooster,
or a male chicken.

Read a Diagram

How is the life cycle
of a panda different
from the life cycle of
a chicken?

 Science in Motion Watch animals
grow at **www.macmillanmh.com**

FACT It takes 9 months for baby humans to grow before they
are born. It takes 4 months for a baby panda to grow.

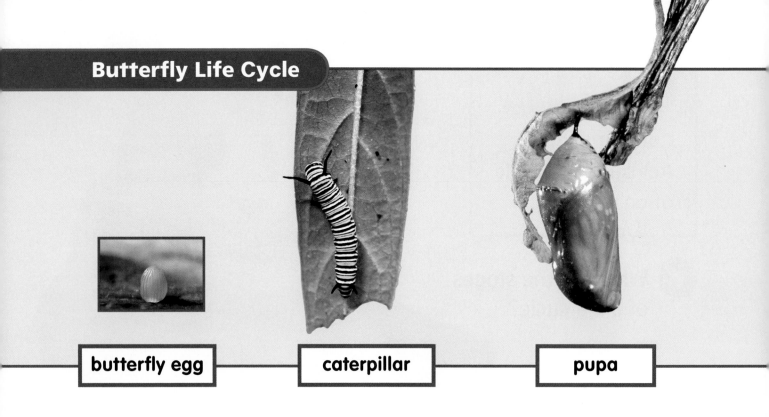

butterfly egg

caterpillar

pupa

What are some other animal life cycles?

Animals such as butterflies, frogs, and crabs do not start out looking like their parents. They change during their lives.

Butterflies begin as eggs. The next stage after an egg hatches is called the **larva**. A caterpillar is the larva of the butterfly. Caterpillars eat plants to grow.

When a caterpillar is ready to change, it stops moving. Its skin becomes a hard shell. Inside the shell, the caterpillar is slowly changing. This is the **pupa** stage. Soon a butterfly comes out of the shell.

young butterfly

adult butterfly

 How does a caterpillar become a butterfly?

Think, Talk, and Write

1. **Predict.** What will the butterfly do when it is an adult?

2. How is the life cycle of a panda the same as the life cycle of a human?

3. Write and draw an example of a life cycle.

Social Studies Link*

Research how long five different animals live. Make a chart to put them in order.

LOG ON **e-Review** Summaries and quizzes online at **www.macmillanmh.com**

Meet Nancy Simmons

Nancy Simmons is a scientist at the American Museum of Natural History. She studies bats all around the world. She has found more than 80 different kinds of bats in one forest. Nancy learns about what bats eat and where they live.

Nancy Simmons is holding a false vampire bat. It is one of the largest bats in the world.

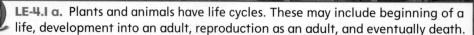

LE-4.1 a. Plants and animals have life cycles. These may include beginning of a life, development into an adult, reproduction as an adult, and eventually death.

Bats give birth to one baby at a time. The baby is called a pup. The pup is small and pink. It has no hair. To stay safe, the pup hangs on to its mother. The pup gets milk from its mother and grows bigger. After a few months the pup is ready to fly.

Soon the young bat leaves its mother. It can find its own food and start its own family.

Bats hang upside down.

Talk About It

Predict. What will happen to a hairless bat pup as it grows?

AMERICAN MUSEUM OF NATURAL HISTORY

Staying Alive

Look and Wonder

This chameleon searches for food every day. How can it keep from being food for other animals?

LE-3.I (a). Describe how the structures of plants and animals complement the environment of the plant or animal. **LE-5.I (b).** Describe basic life functions of common living specimens.... **LE-5.2 (d,e).** Describe some survival behaviors of common living specimens.

How does the color of an animal keep it safe?

You need

scissors

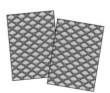

2 pieces of patterned paper

stopwatch

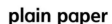

plain paper

What to Do

1. Cut one piece of patterned paper into eight shapes.

2. Put the eight shapes on the other sheet of patterned paper.

3. Time your partner while he or she picks up the shapes.

4. Now put the shapes on plain paper and time your partner again.

5. Which was easier to find? Which was faster? Why?

Explore More

6. **Infer.** How would the activity be different if the shapes were placed on solid colored paper?

Step 1

Why do animals act and look the way they do?

Animals have adaptations to help them stay alive. An **adaptation** is a body part or a way an animal acts that helps it stay alive.

◀ Giraffes have long necks that help them reach leaves in the tops of trees.

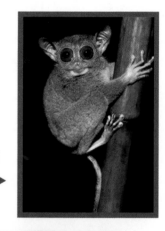

A tarsier has big eyes to see at night and long fingers to dig for food. ▶

An anteater can reach insects underground with its long snout. ▶

Camouflage is a way that animals blend into their surroundings. The color or shape of an animal helps it hide. Camouflage keeps animals from being seen by their enemies.

Ptarmigan Feathers

In summer, a ptarmigan has brown feathers.

In fall, the bird's feathers begin to turn white.

In winter, its feathers blend with the snow.

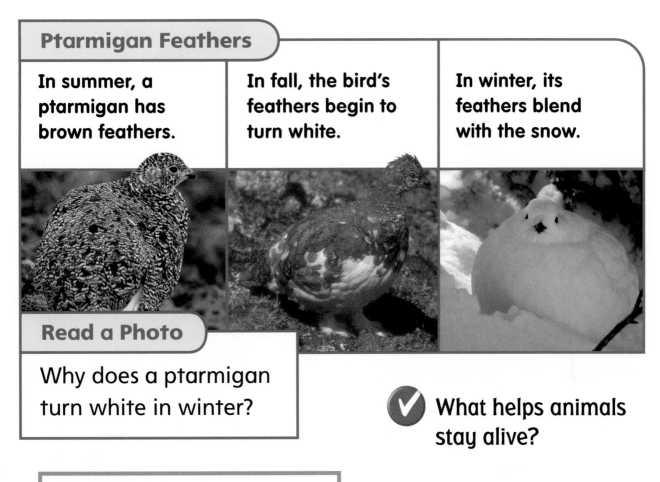

Read a Photo

Why does a ptarmigan turn white in winter?

✓ What helps animals stay alive?

The pattern of a snow leopard is hard to see against the rocks.

How do animals stay safe?

There are many different ways that animals act to stay safe. Some animals stay in large groups. Others leave their homes in winter to be in a warm place and to find food.

▲ Sandhill cranes fly south for the winter.

◀ Some animals, like this dormouse, sleep during the cold winter.

Swimming in a large group helps protect these fish from getting eaten by bigger fish.

Animals have body parts to keep them safe. Some animals have shells or smells to protect them from other animals.

 What are some ways animals protect themselves?

Quick Lab

Investigate to find out why eyes are where they are on different animals.

◀ **Turtles stay safe by hiding in their shells.**

Think, Talk, and Write

1. **Cause and Effect.** How does the white fur of a polar bear help it stay alive?

2. Why is it helpful for fish to stay in a group?

3. Write about one adaptation of an animal that keeps it safe.

Health Link

Draw pictures or talk about how you stay safe.

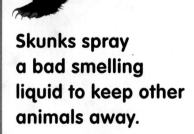

Skunks spray a bad smelling liquid to keep other animals away.

LOG ON **e-Review** Summaries and quizzes online at www.macmillanmh.com

Helpful Traits

Animals have traits that help them live in their environments. Ants have powerful jaws that help them bite and carry food. Frogs have strong legs that help them swim and hop.

angler fish

hummingbird

✏ Write About It

Describe one of the animals above. Where does it live? What do you think it eats? What traits help it live in its environment?

Remember
When you describe, you give details about something.

 e–Journal Write about it online at **www.macmillanmh.com**

 LE-3.la. Each animal has different structures that serve different functions of growth, survival, and reproduction....

Parts of a Group

This dog had 5 puppies. Even though the puppies share many traits, they look different from each other. In this family, 3 of the 5 puppies are brown. You can write this as the fraction $\frac{3}{5}$.

Write Fractions

How many of the 5 puppies are black? Write a fraction to show your answer.

Now draw a group of 3 puppies. Make one third of the group brown.

Remember

You can use a fraction to tell about parts of a group.

MI.Ib. Select the appropriate operation to solve mathematical problems
MI.Ic. Apply mathematical skills to describe the natural world

83
EXTEND

So Many Animals!

There are so many kinds of animals! They are alike in many ways. They need food, water, air, and a place to live. Their body parts help them get what they need to stay alive.

Animals are different in many ways, too. Fish have fins to swim and gills to breathe. Birds have feathers to keep warm. Mammals have hair on their bodies and breathe with lungs.

Animals grow in many ways. Some lay eggs. Some give birth to live babies. All of them will grow to look like their parents.

Animals have many ways to keep safe. Some move together in big groups. Others use their colors or shapes to help hide. In the animal world, keeping safe means staying alive!

CHAPTER 2 Review

Vocabulary

Use each word once for items 1–5.

adaptation
amphibian
larva
life cycle
mammal

1. An animal that lives the first part of its life in water and another part on land is an _____.
   LE-4.1 (b,e)

2. An animal that feeds milk to its young is a _____.
   LE-1.1 (a); LE-3.1 (a)

3. How an animal grows and changes is called its _____.
   LE-4.1 (a,c,e,f)

4. This caterpillar is a _____.
   LE-4.1 (e)

5. The blubber of a whale keeps it warm. An _____ like this helps an animal stay alive where it lives.
   LE-3.1 (a,c)

Answer the questions below.

6. Classify. How would you classify these two animals? List their traits.

LE-2.2 (a); LE-3.1 (c)

7. Predict. What will happen when a chick hatches from an egg?

LE-4.1 (f); LE-4.2 (a)

8. Put these pictures of a frog life cycle in order.

LE-4.1 (e,f); LE-4.2 (a)

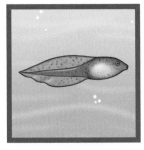

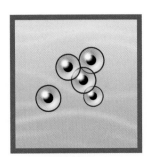

| tadpole | adult frog | eggs | tadpole with legs |

9. What are some ways animals can keep safe?

LE-3.1 (a); LE-5.1 (b); LE-5.2 (c,d,e)

The Big Idea

10. How do animals grow and change?

LE-3; LE-4; LE-5

CHAPTER 3

Looking at Habitats

The **Big Idea**

What are habitats?

beavers making a dam in Wyoming

Key Vocabulary

habitat a place where plants and animals live

(page 94)

predator an animal that hunts other animals for food

(page 103)

drought a long period of time with little or no rain

(page 110)

fossil what is left of a living thing from the past

(page 114)

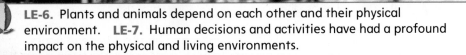

LE-6. Plants and animals depend on each other and their physical environment. **LE-7.** Human decisions and activities have had a profound impact on the physical and living environments.

Places to Live

reef fish in the Bahamas

Look and Wonder

What can you tell about the place these plants and animals live?

LE-6.I (b). Describe how plants and animals, including humans, depend upon each other and the nonliving environment.

Where do animals live?

What to Do

1 **Observe.** Look at the footprints below. What animal do you think made them?

2 **Infer.** How does the shape of its feet help this animal? Share your idea with a partner.

3 Draw a picture of the animal and the place where it lives.

Explore More

4 **Communicate.** What other animals could live near this animal? What do they need to live? How do they get food and water? Make a chart.

You need

paper

crayons

What is a habitat?

A **habitat** is a place where plants and animals live. In a habitat, animals can find the food, homes, and water they need to live. Plants need soil, rain, sunlight, and animals in their habitats to live.

grassy and warm

cold and snowy

wet and grassy

There are many kinds of habitats. Some have lots of rain. Some are dry. Some places are windy and others are cold.

Different plants and animals need different habitats to live. These pictures show some kinds of habitats.

 What are some kinds of habitats?

hot and dry

How do living things use their habitats?

Animals use the plants living in their habitat for food. Some animals eat other animals that live in the same habitat. Animals also use their habitat to hide and sleep.

Animals such as moles dig tunnels in the soil to find food and shelter. Some insects make their homes under rocks.

Forest Habitat

Read a Diagram

How do the squirrel and the snake use their habitat?

Different plants need different kinds of soil to live. Some plants grow in sandy soil and some plants grow in rocky soil.

Plants that live in dry places can hold water. Plants that live in very wet places can get rid of extra water. They have leaves that point down so water can roll off them.

 How do animals and plants use their habitats?

Quick Lab

Find a picture of a habitat. Draw and write to **communicate** what could live there.

This plant lives in a dry place. Its leaves store water. ▶

Think, Talk, and Write

1. Summarize. How are habitats different?

2. How do plants survive in their habitat?

3. Write about a hot, dry habitat. Describe what you would find there.

Art Link

Draw a picture of a habitat you want to visit. How would you get what you need there?

 e-Review Summaries and quizzes online at **www.macmillanmh.com**

Inquiry Skill: Put Things in Order

When you **put things in order**, you tell what happens first, next, and last.

▶ Learn It

Think about how a plant grows. Then look at the pictures and put them in order. You can use a chart to help you tell the order.

The plant gets bigger.

A seedling grows.

I plant a seed.

I plant a seed.	→	?	→	?
first		**next**		**last**

▶ **Try It**

Look at the pictures below.

beaver dam and pond

beaver cutting trees

stream in the woods

1. What picture comes first? next? last?

2. Write About It. Write about what happens to the stream and woods when beavers build a dam.

 S3.la. Accurately transfer data from a science journal or notes to appropriate graphic organizer

Food Chains and Food Webs

Look and Wonder

Animals need food to live.
What do different animals eat?

LE-6.I (c). Describe how plants and animals, including humans, depend upon each other and the nonliving environment. **LE-6.2 (b).** Describe the relationship of the Sun as an energy source for living and nonliving cycles.

What do animals eat?

What to Do

You need

① The Sun makes plants grow. Which animals eat plants? Which animals eat those animals?

paper strips

crayons

② Draw the Sun on the yellow strip. Draw some grass and trees on the green strip. Then draw a bird on the red strip and a grasshopper on the brown strip.

glue

③ **Put Things in Order.** Make a chain of strips. Glue them in their order as food.

④ **Communicate.** Describe the order of your chain with a partner.

Explore More

⑤ Repeat the activity with three other animals. Communicate how you put the animals in order.

Vocabulary

food chain

predator

prey

food web

What is a food chain?

A **food chain** is a model of the order in which living things get the food they need. Most food chains start with the Sun.

There are many food chains. Some are on land and some are in the water. Some can be both on land and in water!

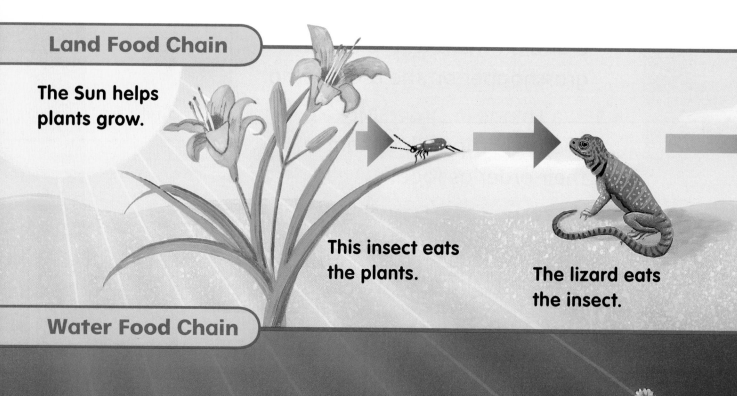

Land Food Chain

The Sun helps plants grow.

This insect eats the plants.

The lizard eats the insect.

Water Food Chain

The Sun helps plankton grow.

Krill eat plankton.

A sea horse eats the krill.

Animals can eat plants or other animals. An animal that hunts other animals for food is a **predator**. Animals that are hunted by predators are called **prey**.

Some animals eat plants and animals that are dead. Animals such as worms break the dead things up into very small pieces.

Quick Lab

Communicate. Act out a food chain with puppets.

✓ Where can food chains be found?

The snake eats the lizard.

The hawk eats the snake.

Large fish, such as tuna, eat sea horses.

Sharks eat large fish.

A Desert Food Web

Arrows in the food web go from food to eater.

Read a Diagram

What are the different food chains in this food web?

LOG ON *Science in Motion* See the parts of a food web at **www.macmillanmh.com**

What is a food web?

A **food web** is two or more food chains that are connected. Sometimes one kind of animal is food for many animals. Mice are eaten by hawks, owls, and snakes.

Animals also eat more than one kind of animal. Hawks eat mice, rabbits, frogs, and snakes. If you put those food chains together, you have a food web.

 What are some other predators and their prey?

The insect is prey for the bird.

Think, Talk, and Write

1. **Main Idea and Details.** Describe an example of a food chain.

2. What is a food web?

3. Write about how you are part of a food chain.

Health Link

Think of a healthy lunch. Show how your meal is part of a food web. Draw the web.

LOG ON **e-Review** Summaries and quizzes online at **www.macmillanmh.com**

Writing in Science

A Food Web for Lunch

Emma is having a chicken sandwich for lunch. She drew a food web to show how each food is related.

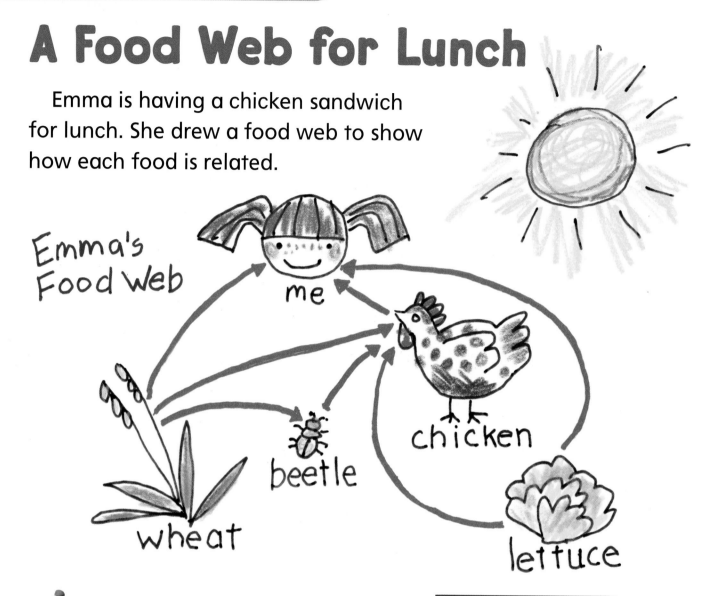

Emma's Food Web

me

beetle

chicken

wheat

lettuce

✏️ **Write About It**

Explain how Emma, the chicken, lettuce, and wheat form a food web. Think about the food chains in Emma's lunch to help you form a food web of your own lunch.

Remember
When you are writing to explain, you tell the steps in order.

LOG ON 🔵 e-Journal Write about it online at www.macmillanmh.com

 M2.lb. Explain verbally, graphically, or in writing patterns and relationships observed in the physical and living environment

Food for a Toad

Most animals eat different foods to stay alive.

Problem Solving

A toad ate 3 grasshoppers on Monday. It ate 5 ants on Tuesday. It ate 4 crickets on Wednesday. How many animals did the toad eat in all?

Remember

Making a sketch can help solve problems. Think about whether you need to add or subtract.

M2.Ia. Explain verbally, graphically, or in writing the reasoning used to develop mathematical conclusions

Habitats Change

Doylestown, Pennsylvania

Look and Wonder

Does your habitat always look the same? How does it change?

LE-6.I (f). Describe how plants and animals, including humans, depend upon each other and the nonliving environment. **LE-7.I (a).** Identify ways in which humans have changed their environment and the effects of those changes.

What happens when habitats change?

What to Do

1. On a large sheet of paper, draw a large meadow, woods, and river.

2. Place the animals where they would live.

3. Use blocks as houses and buildings. Build a town with houses and stores.

4. **Observe.** What happens to the meadow, woods, and animals that live there?

5. **Infer.** How does building a town affect the animals, meadow, woods, farms, river, and people?

Explore More

6. **Predict.** What will happen if a highway is built?

You need

large pieces of paper

crayons

small toys and blocks

Step 2

Vocabulary

drought

endangered

fossil

extinct

SCIENCE QUEST Explore fossils with the Treasure Hunters.

How do habitats change?

Nature can change habitats in many ways. A **drought** is a long period of time when there is little or no rain. Plants and animals can not live without water. Floods or fires can also change habitats.

Drought

Read a Photo

How does a drought change a habitat?

Animals can change habitats. Beavers make dams. The dam can make a pond.

People can change habitats, too. People build houses and other buildings where grass, plants, and trees were growing.

▲ **Bulldozers help people clear land to build on. Clearing the land changes the habitat.**

 How can a habitat change?

The beaver dam blocks the water from the stream and forms a pond.

What happens when habitats change?

When a habitat is changed, animals may not be able to find the things they need. Some animals may die. When many of one kind of animal die and only a few are left, that animal is **endangered**. All these animals are endangered.

⌁Quick Lab

Draw a comic strip about a habitat. **Communicate** how habitats can change.

whooping crane

tigers

People hunt tigers for their fur and cut down their forest homes.

People built over the marshes where cranes live.

Animals can become endangered when people hunt them or build on their habitats.

When habitats change, some animals have adaptations that help them live in their new habitat. Animals may find new places to get food and live.

 Why do animals become endangered?

manatee

People have taken over many rivers where manatees live. Fishing nets and powerboats also hurt manatees.

FACT ▶ People helped American alligators survive so they are not endangered anymore.

How can we tell what a habitat used to be like?

Scientists study fossils to learn about Earth's past. A **fossil** is what is left of a living thing from the past. Scientists get clues about habitats of the past from the plant and animal fossils they find.

Some fossils do not match the habitat they were found in. Then scientists can tell that the habitat has changed.

Look at the fossil found here. What do you think the habitat used to be?

How do you think this animal moved? Why?

Some plants and animals that lived long ago still live today. Some have died out, or become **extinct**. Now we only have their fossils. Fossils can help tell how animals may have looked or moved.

 What can fossils tell us about habitats long ago?

Think, Talk, and Write

1. **Cause and Effect.** What happens to plants and animals when their habitat changes?

2. What are some ways animals can stay alive when their habitat changes?

3. Write about how people can change habitats and what might happen to animals and plants.

Art Link

Make a poster about endangered animals.

LOG ON e-**Review** Summaries and quizzes online at www.macmillanmh.com

Meet Mike Novacek

Mike Novacek grew up in Southern California. When he was young he visited the La Brea Tar Pits in Los Angeles. He loved to learn about the fossils he saw there. He learned about animals that lived long ago.

Mike Novacek

▼ **Mike travels to the Gobi Desert in China to look for new fossils.**

Asia

Gobi Desert

United States

New York

Los Angeles

S3.1a. Accurately transfer data from a science journal or notes to appropriate graphic organizer

Today Mike is a scientist at the American Museum of Natural History in New York. He travels all around the world to collect fossils. He looks for fossils of reptiles, mammals, and dinosaurs. Many of these animals lived 80 million years ago!

Mike and his team went to the Gobi Desert to look for fossils. They found fossils of the Kryptobaatar. These were tiny mammals the size of a mouse. These mammals lived at the same time and place as dinosaurs!

Mike studies fossils to find out about the past.

Talk About It

Cause and Effect. What made Mike want to study fossils?

▲ **Kryptobaatar skull**

AMERICAN
MUSEUM ᵒᶠ
NATURAL
HISTORY

Changing Habitats

This is a woodland forest habitat. Deer, birds, fish, and snakes live here. There are many kinds of plants and trees here, too. What would happen if this habitat changed?

Oh no! A fire is coming! Deer run away. Snakes slither out from under rocks. Birds fly far from the smoke. Most of the animals can stay safe away from the fire.

The fire is over. Some plants
burned. Some plants survived. New
plants like fireweed and grasses
grow quickly. These plants have
more room to grow after the fire.
They can also get more sunlight.

The animals come back and
eat the new plants. Deer love
the soft new leaves. A snake
slithers back under a rock. The
birds fly back to the trees that
survived. Foxes make a new den.

121

Vocabulary

Use each word once for items 1–5.

1. When there are not many of one kind of animal left, the animal is called _____.
   LE-6.1 (f)

2. When it does not rain for a long time there is a _____.
   LE-1.1 (a,b)

3. A place where animals and plants live together is called a _____.

4. The grasshopper in this picture is the _____.
   LE-6.1 (b,c)

5. The picture below shows part of a _____.
   LE-6.1 (b,c)

drought

endangered

food chain

habitat

prey

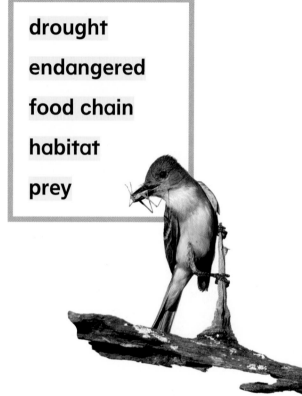

Answer the questions below.

6. **Summarize.** How do plants and animals use each other?
LE-6.I (a,b,c); LE-6.2 (a)

7. Compare the pictures below. How are they different? What do you think happened?
LE-I.I (b); LE-6.2 (a)

8. **Put Things in Order.** Put this food chain in order.
LE-6.I (b,c); LE-6.2 (a,b)

| rabbit | Sun | fox | grass |

9. What happens to animals and plants when habitats change?
LE-6.I (e,f)

10. What are habitats?
LE-6; LE-7

Literature
Poem

The Seed

by Aileen Fisher

How does it know,
this little seed,
if it is to grow
to a flower or weed,
if it is to be
a vine or shoot,
or grow to a tree
with a long deep root?
A seed is so small,
where do you suppose
it stores up all
of the things it knows?

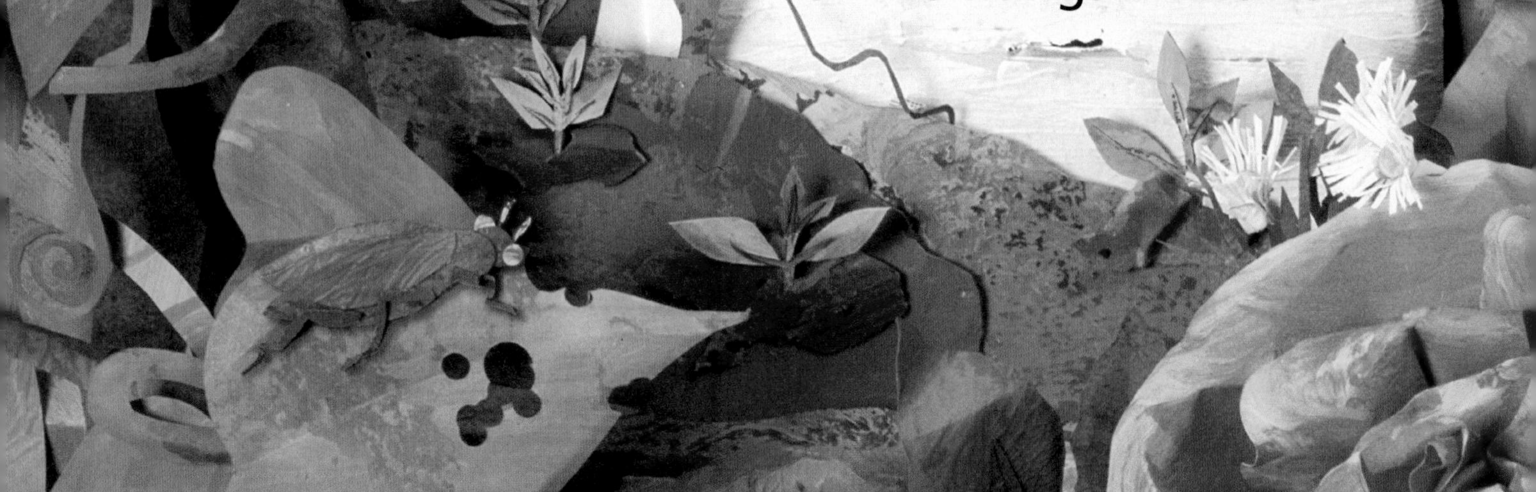

Talk About It

What do you know about seeds?

Bird Bander

Do you love to learn about birds? You could become a bird bander. A bird bander helps scientists keep track of birds.

The bander catches a bird and puts a tiny band around its ankle. This band has a number on it, and the bander writes it down. The bander also writes the bird's age and size.

Then the bander returns the bird to the wild. Later, other banders and scientists might trap the same bird. They can look up the bird's number and see how it grew and changed.

bird bander

More Careers to Think About

wildlife guide

veterinarian

LOG ON e-Careers at www.macmillanmh.com

Earth Science

One million cloud droplets make one raindrop.

Watching the Weather

Doppler radar dome

Weather Everyday

Is it sunny outside? Could it rain this afternoon? How do you know what the weather will be today? Weather is the condition of the air around us. The National Weather Service (NWS) observes the weather and predicts changes.

Extreme Weather

Scientists at the NWS in Buffalo, New York, observe the weather. They measure and keep track of air temperature, wind speed, and wind direction. They also use special tools to take pictures of clouds.

Scientists use the data to predict extreme changes in the weather. These big changes can cause dangerous storms. You can stay safe if you know about extreme weather!

Think, Talk, and Write

Critical Thinking Why is it important to keep track of weather?

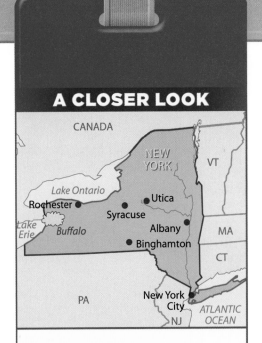

A CLOSER LOOK

Main Idea
Knowing about weather can keep you safe.

Activity

Observe What is the weather like in your neighborhood?

■ Observe the weather at your school each day for a week. Make a table to keep track of your observations.

 PS-2.lb. Weather can be described and measured by: temperature; wind speed and direction; form and amount of precipitation; general sky conditions (cloudy, sunny, partly cloudy).

New York Apples

pick your own apples

Apple Picking

Have you ever picked an apple right off a tree? You can at an apple orchard. New York is known for apples. There are many orchards south of Lake Ontario. The lake causes cool nights in summer and fall. Apples grow very well in this weather.

Changing Seasons, Changing Apples

Spring brings warmer weather and rain to New York. Apple trees start to grow flowers. Summer weather is warm with lots of sunshine. The flowers grow into apples.

Apples become ready to eat in the fall. Cool fall nights help the apples stay fresh and juicy. Winter weather is cold. Apple trees rest, or go dormant, until winter is over.

Think, Talk, and Write

Critical Thinking What would happen if you picked apples during the summer?

A CLOSER LOOK

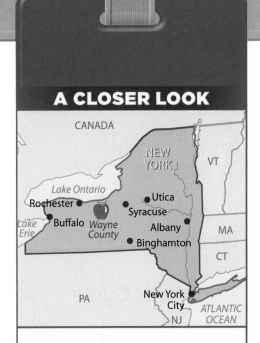

▶ **Main Idea**

The weather changes as seasons change.

▶ **Activity**

Compare Draw a picture of another tree that grows fruit.

■ Show how the tree changes in spring, summer, fall, and winter.

■ How is it like an apple tree? How is it different?

131

Observing Weather

The Big Idea

How can we describe weather?

Key Vocabulary

More Vocabulary

anemometer, page 139

evaporate, page 144

condense, page 145

cirrus, page 153

temperature a measurement of how hot or cold something is (page 136)

precipitation water falling from the sky as rain, snow, or hail (page 137)

cumulus large, white, puffy clouds (page 152)

stratus thin clouds that form into layers like sheets (page 153)

PS-I. The Earth and celestial phenomena can be described by principles of relative motion and perspective. **PS-2.** Many of the phenomena that we observe on Earth involve interactions among components of air, water, and land. **LE-6.** Plants and animals depend on each other and their physical environment.

Weather

Look and Wonder

Weather changes from day to day. How can you describe this kind of weather?

PS-2.I (a,b). Describe the relationship among air, water, and land on Earth.

Inquiry Activity

How does the weather change each day?

You need

thermometer

construction paper

What to Do

1. Make a chart with these columns at the top: Date, Temperature, Weather.

2. **Record Data.** Observe the weather each day. Record on the chart what you see. Draw any clouds you see.

3. **Compare.** After several days, compare how the weather changed from day to day.

Explore More

4. Add a column to your chart called Wind. Record how wind changes from day to day.

Step 2

S3.Ia. Accurately transfer data from a science journal or notes to appropriate graphic organizer

Vocabulary

temperature

precipitation

anemometer

What is weather?

When you get dressed in the morning, you might think about the weather. How hot or cold will it be outside? Is it a sunny day, or is it raining or snowing?

One way that people describe weather is by the temperature. **Temperature** describes how hot or cold something is.

This thermometer shows 70 degrees Fahrenheit (70°F) or 21 degrees Celsius (21°C).

This thermometer shows 40°F or 5°C. It is cooler, so you must dress warmly.

Another way people describe weather is by telling if it is raining. Rain, snow, sleet, and hail are all kinds of precipitation. **Precipitation** is water that falls to Earth from clouds. Each kind of precipitation can be measured in a different way.

 How can you talk about weather?

Hail is chunks of ice that fall from thunderclouds.

A ruler is used to measure the depth of snow.

A rain gauge is used to measure the amount of rain that falls in one spot.

What is wind?

All around Earth there is hot and cold air. Differences between hot and cold air cause the air to move, making wind.

Wind can be strong or light. One way to measure how the wind is blowing is with a wind sock. Wind blows into the open end of a wind sock and makes it point in the direction the wind is blowing.

If the wind sock moves gently, the wind is light. If it blows out straight, the wind is strong. ▶

≡Quick Lab

Make a wind sock. **Observe** how strong the wind is.

Wind Sock

Read a Photo

How strong is the wind in this photograph?

People also measure the wind's speed with an **anemometer**. The cups on the anemometer catch the wind and spin. The stronger the wind is, the faster the cups spin. The anemometer keeps track of how many times the cups spin.

This scientist is using an anemometer. ▶

 How can we measure wind?

Think, Talk, and Write

1. **Summarize.** How do anemometers and wind socks measure wind?

2. What are some different kinds of weather?

3. Write about and draw the different kinds of precipitation.

Social Studies Link

Research what the weather is like in another country. How is it like your weather? How is it different?

LOG ON ⓔ-**Review** Summaries and quizzes online at www.macmillanmh.com

A Snowy Day

What are these people doing on this snowy day?

✏ Write About It

Write a story about what you might do on a snowy day. Use the photograph to help you think about what a snowy day might be like.

Remember

A story has a beginning, middle, and end. A story uses describing words.

 e–Journal Write about it online at **www.macmillanmh.com**

 S3.3a. Explain their findings to others, and actively listen to suggestions for possible interpretations and ideas

A Sunny Day

Look carefully at the thermometer. What is the temperature in degrees Fahrenheit (°F)?

Write a Number Sentence

The weatherman predicted that the temperature will rise to 55 degrees Fahrenheit (55°F). Write a number sentence to show how many degrees Fahrenheit it will rise.

Remember

The left side of the thermometer shows Fahrenheit.

 M2.1b. Explain verbally, graphically, or in writing patterns and relationships observed in the physical and living environment

The Water Cycle

Torres del Paine National Park, Chile

Look and Wonder

Where do you see water in this picture?

 PS-1.1 (b). Describe patterns of daily, monthly, and seasonal changes in their environment.   **LE-6.2 (c).** Describe the relationship of the Sun as an energy source for living and nonliving cycles.

Where did the water go?

What to Do

You need

2 cups

1. Fill both cups halfway with water. Mark the water levels.

plastic wrap

2. Cover one cup with plastic wrap. Tape it to the cup. Place both cups in a sunny place.

water

3. **Predict.** How will the levels of water change in each cup over several days?

4. **Record Data.** Write what you see in each cup every day.

tape

5. **Draw Conclusions.** What happened to the water levels after several days? Why?

marker

Explore More

6. What would happen if you used twice as much water? Try it.

Step 2

S3.4a. State, orally and in writing, any inferences or generalizations indicated by the data, with appropriate modifications of their original prediction/explanation

143
EXPLORE

How does water disappear?

When you jump into a swimming pool you feel the water on your body. This water is liquid.

But water is not always liquid. When water heats up, some of it changes into a gas we cannot see. Water can **evaporate**, or change from a liquid to a gas. The gas travels in the air as water vapor.

Liquid water from the pond evaporates into water vapor in the air.

FACT Clouds form everywhere, not just over water.

These clouds are made of droplets of water.

water vapor

Water vapor rises in warm air. As the air cools, it can no longer hold the water vapor. So the water changes again!

This time, the water vapor will **condense**, or turn back into liquid. The water forms into tiny droplets. Sometimes these droplets form clouds.

How can water change forms?

What is the water cycle?

Water evaporates from oceans, rivers, and lakes. Then the water condenses into clouds and falls as precipitation. We call these changes the water cycle. All over Earth, water is always moving through the water cycle.

 How does water vapor move back down to Earth?

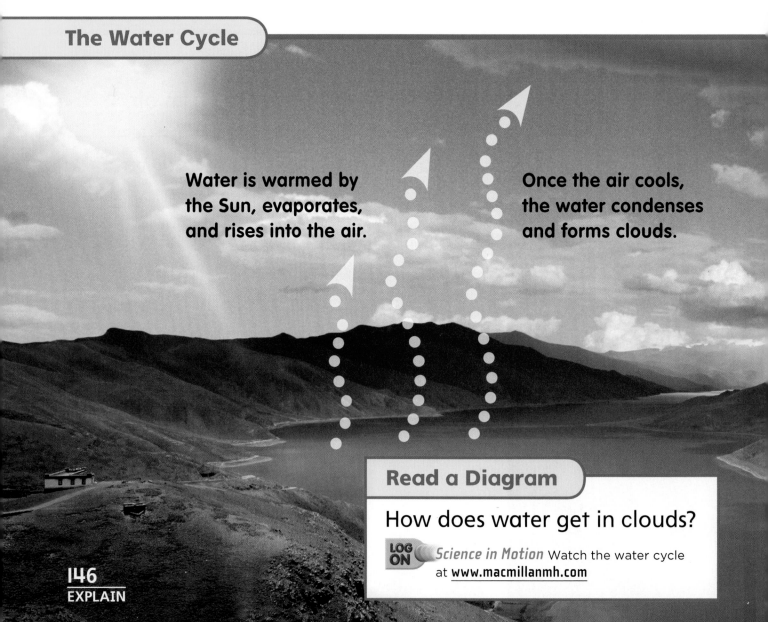

The Water Cycle

Water is warmed by the Sun, evaporates, and rises into the air.

Once the air cools, the water condenses and forms clouds.

Read a Diagram

How does water get in clouds?

LOG ON *Science in Motion* Watch the water cycle at www.macmillanmh.com

Think, Talk, and Write

1. **Cause and Effect.** What happens in the water cycle?

2. What happens when water evaporates?

3. Write about how water changes when it evaporates and condenses.

Music Link*

Write a song about water vapor and clouds.

LOG ON e-Review Summaries and quizzes online at **www.macmillanmh.com**

Precipitation can fall as rain, snow, sleet, or hail.

Over time, rain and melted snow flow back to the lakes, rivers, and oceans.

Inquiry Skill: Predict

When you **predict**, you use what you know to tell what you think will happen.

▶ **Learn It**

Kendra needs to decide which footwear she should wear outside. What do you think she will choose?

What I Know	What I Predict
I know it's raining outside.	I predict that Kendra will wear her rain boots.

▶ **Try It**

1. Look through this window and at the thermometer. What type of weather do you think is coming?

2. What information did you use to help you predict?

3. Write About It. What do you need to wear to keep warm on a cold day? Write a story about it.

S3.1a. Accurately transfer data from a science journal or notes to appropriate graphic organizer

Changes in Weather

Owens Valley, California

Look and Wonder

Look at the sky. Did you know that clouds can help predict weather?

 **PS-I.I (b).** Describe patterns of daily, monthly, and seasonal changes in their environment.

How can clouds help predict the weather?

What to Do

1 **Observe.** Look carefully at the sky every day this week.

2 **Record Data.** Draw the kinds of clouds you see each day for a week. Write the date next to each picture. Then predict what the weather will be like tomorrow.

3 The next day, record what the weather is like. Draw the clouds and the date. Was your prediction from the day before correct?

4 **Draw Conclusions.** How can clouds help predict weather?

←mostly blue sky

puffy clouds with dark purple edges.

our house

Tuesday, March 10.

I predict it will rain.

What happened: I was right. It rained!

Explore More

5 **Predict.** Write a weather report for the next week. Why is tomorrow's weather the easiest day to predict?

S3.1. Organize observations and measurements of objects and events through classification and the preparation of simple charts and tables. **S3.3a.** Explain their findings to others, and actively listen to suggestions for possible interpretations and ideas

What are different kinds of clouds?

Not all clouds look the same. There are different kinds of clouds. Each means a different type of weather may be coming.

Cumulus clouds are small, white puffs. Cumulus clouds may appear in long, rippled rows.

▼ Cumulus clouds are often seen in spring and summer. Small, puffy cumulus clouds mean good weather.

FACT ▷ Not all clouds are rain clouds.

▲ When you see cirrus clouds, it usually means that the weather will change within the next day.

Cirrus clouds are thin clouds very high in the sky. They are made of ice. The wind blows cirrus clouds into wispy streams.

Stratus clouds are often low in the sky. They come in sheets and cover the entire sky. Stratus clouds can be thick or thin.

 Which cloud type is best for the day of a picnic?

▲ When you see stratus clouds, it usually means that a storm with rain or snow is coming.

How can we stay safe from weather?

When different types of air come together, the weather changes. Storm clouds can grow thick and lightning can form in them.

Stay safe in dangerous weather. Pay attention to weather reports. During storms, do not go outside near tall objects where lightning may strike.

Quick Lab

Use a paper bag to **make a model** of a thunder sound.

Lightning Safety

Avoid open spaces.

Stay out of water.

Do not stand under trees.

Stay indoors.

Read a Chart

Where should you go in a storm?

Sometimes storms become very strong. They can turn into hurricanes and cause disasters. Strong thunderstorms can make spinning columns of air called tornadoes.

Tornadoes can pick up large objects from the ground and damage property.

 How can weather change?

Think, Talk, and Write

1. **Main Idea and Details.** How can clouds help people predict the weather?

2. What kinds of clouds predict a storm is coming?

3. Draw and write about a storm you have seen.

Social Studies Link

Make a short skit or commercial showing how to prepare for severe weather.

LOG ON e-**Review** Summaries and quizzes online at **www.macmillanmh.com**

Predicting Storms

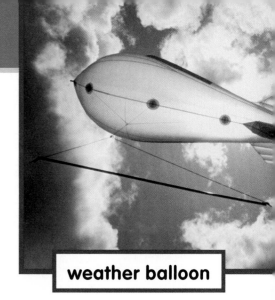

weather balloon

Even on a sunny day, dangerous thunderstorms can happen quickly. Knowing that a storm is coming is very useful. If there is lightning, you would know to stay inside and not use electricity.

If there is a flood, you would know what to do. You can go to a higher floor in your home. How do scientists predict storms?

S3.Ia. Accurately transfer data from a science journal or notes to appropriate graphic organizer

1892: Weather balloons are first used. Weather balloons can float high above Earth. As the balloons travel, they collect data about wind and weather conditions that might lead to storms.

▼ **Doppler radar**

Mid-1990's: Doppler radar is widely used. Radar is a tool that sends out radio waves into the air. The waves hit things in the air, such as raindrops. Then the waves come back. The data is recorded. Doppler radar can measure how fast a storm is moving and where the storm is going.

▲ **Doppler radar recorded this image of a hurricane.**

Talk About It

Main Idea and Details. How do scientists predict the weather?

Earth's Water Cycle

There is a lot of water on Earth! There is water in oceans, rivers, and ponds. When water on Earth warms, some evaporates, or turns into water vapor. Water vapor rises in the air.

When water vapor cools, it
forms clouds. There are many
types of clouds. Some are thick
and some are thin. Some are high
in the sky and some are low.

When clouds get heavy,
precipitation falls to Earth.
Precipitation can be rain, hail,
sleet, or snow. There can be
storms with lightning and thunder.
Look out, a storm is coming!

The storm is over now. The rain has stopped falling. The ground is still wet, but the Sun is coming out. The Sun will warm Earth's water and start the cycle again.

Vocabulary

Use each word once for items 1–6.

condense
cumulus
evaporate
precipitation
stratus
temperature

1. When water vapor starts to _____ it turns into a liquid.
PS-3.1 (g); PS-3.2 (b)

2. The _____ tells how hot or cold it is.
PS-2.1 (a,b)

3. Rain and snow are kinds of _____.
PS-2.1 (b,c)

4. Small, white puffy clouds are called _____ clouds.

5. You can see the Sun through these _____ clouds.

6. Water can _____. It becomes water vapor and goes into the air.
PS-2.1 (c); PS-4.1 (d)

Answer the questions below.

7. Predict. Look at the photo. What kind of weather is coming?
PS-2.I (a,b)

8. Summarize. Describe the water cycle.
PS-2.I (c); LE-6.2 (c)

9. What do clouds tell us about weather?
PS-2.I (a,b)

10. What tools can we use to measure weather?
PS-2.I (a,b)

II. How can we describe weather?
PS-I; PS-2; LE-6

CHAPTER 5

Earth and Space

The
**Big
Idea**

What can we see
in the night sky?

a view of Earth from the Moon

Key Vocabulary

axis a center line that an object spins around (page 169)

rotation, page 168

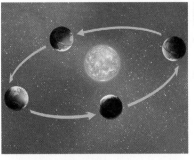

orbit the path Earth takes around the Sun (page 178)

phase the Moon's shape as we see it from Earth (page 187)

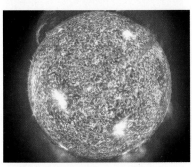

star an object in space made of hot, glowing gases (page 188)

PS-I. The Earth and celestial phenomena can be described by principles of relative motion and perspective.

Day and Night

Santorini, Greece

Look and Wonder

Why do you think the sky gets dark each night?

 PS-1.1 (a,c). Describe patterns of daily, monthly, and seasonal changes in their environment.

Why can't we see the Sun at night?

flashlight

What to Do

① Stand 12 steps away facing a partner.

② Point a flashlight at your partner. The flashlight is the Sun. The partner is Earth.

③ **Predict.** Let your partner turn around slowly in front of the flashlight. Will he or she always be able to see the light? Try it.

④ **Infer.** How does this model show why we can not see the Sun at night?

Step ①

Explore More

⑤ **Make a Model.** What pattern is made when your partner turns around in front of the flashlight three times? Try it.

M2.1b. Explain verbally, graphically, or in writing patterns and relationships observed in the physical and living environment

Vocabulary

rotation

axis

What causes day and night?

Earth spins every moment of the day and night. You do not feel it, but it is happening right now. The spinning of Earth is called **rotation**.

Earth's rotation causes day and night. When one side of Earth faces the Sun, it is day. At the same time, it is night on the other side of Earth.

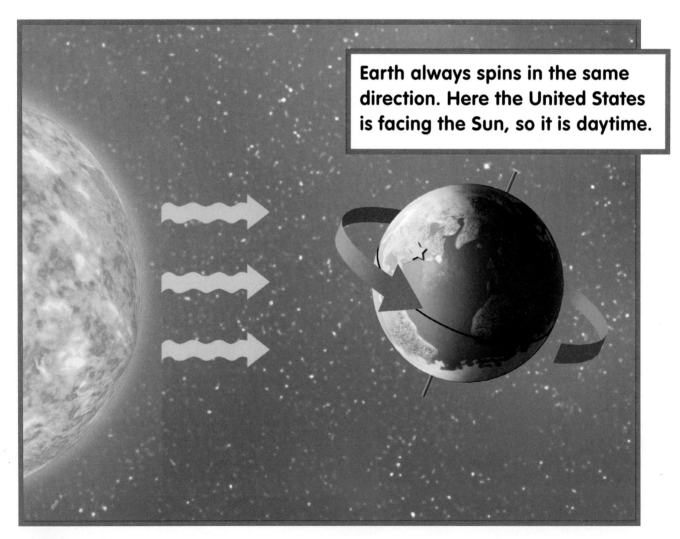

Earth always spins in the same direction. Here the United States is facing the Sun, so it is daytime.

Earth rotates around an imaginary line called an **axis**. The axis goes through the center of Earth from north to south. Every 24 hours, Earth makes one full turn on its axis. This pattern of day and night repeats again and again.

✓ Why can we see sunlight only during the day?

Read a Diagram

Is it day or night in the United States? How do you know?

Earth's Axis

axis

Why do the Sun and Moon seem to move?

We live on Earth and look out toward the sky. As Earth rotates, the Sun and Moon seem to move across the sky.

You can see the Sun make different shadows during the day. As Earth rotates, shadows on the ground change. Longer shadows mean the Sun is lower in the sky.

Quick Lab

Make a flip book of the Moon. **Observe** how the Moon seems to move across the sky in one night.

▼ **The length of the shadow changes as the Sun seems to move across the sky.**

8:00 a.m.

In the morning, the Sun seems to rise in the sky.

12:00 noon

By the middle of the day, we see the Sun high in the sky.

4:00 p.m.

As it gets dark, the Sun seems to set in the sky.

Each night the Moon also seems to move across the sky.

 Why does the Sun appear to move in the sky?

Think, Talk, and Write

1. **Problem and Solution.** How can you tell what time it is if you do not have a watch?

2. What causes day and night?

3. Draw and write about how the Sun or Moon seem to move.

Music Link

Write a song about day and night to the tune of "Twinkle Twinkle Little Star."

 e-Review Summaries and quizzes online at **www.macmillanmh.com**

Inquiry Skill: Draw Conclusions

▶ Learn It

When scientists draw conclusions, they use what they observe to explain what happens.

Linda looks at this picture.

She sees the lights on and the dark sky. Linda has seen some of the houses before. She draws the conclusion that this picture was taken at night in her town.

▶ **Try It**

Observe the lengths of shadows. Then draw conclusions about the time of day.

1. Push a stick straight into a pot of dirt. Place the pot in a sunny spot.

2. Look at the stick at different times of day. Sit in the same spot each time. Draw the Sun, stick, and shadow. Write the time of day on each drawing.

3. Compare. Talk to your partner about how the shadows changed. When was the shadow longest?

4. Draw Conclusions. What does the time of day have to do with the length of shadows?

 M3.Ia. Use appropriate scientific tools, such as metric rulers, spring scale, pan balance, graph paper, thermometers [Fahrenheit and Celsius], graduated cylinder to solve problems about the natural world

Why Seasons Happen

Marshfield, Vermont

Look and Wonder

What time of year is shown here?
How can you tell?

PS-I.I (a,b). Describe patterns of daily, monthly, and seasonal changes in their environment.

What clothes do people wear in each season?

What to Do

1 Write the name of a different season in each corner of your paper.

2 Cut out pictures of different kinds of clothes from magazines.

3 Classify. Glue the pictures near the seasons where they belong.

4 Draw Conclusions. What do people wear in different seasons?

Explore More

5 Classify. Sort your clothes at home by season. Explain how you grouped your clothes.

You need

paper

markers

magazines

scissors

glue stick

Step **2**

S3.3a. Explain their findings to others, and actively listen to suggestions for possible interpretations and ideas

What are the seasons like?

Each season has a different kind of weather. In fall, the air can become cool. Leaves on some trees turn colors and fall off.

In winter the air is cold. In some places it snows. Animals must keep warm. Some birds fly to warmer places. People wear warmer clothes.

▲ There are fewer hours of daylight in fall.

▲ In many places it can snow in winter.

In spring the weather becomes warmer. There are many rainy days. Trees and flowers bloom. Birds return from their winter homes.

Summer is the hottest season. There are more hours of sunlight than of night. What season comes after summer? The seasons start all over again!

▲ **There are many rainy days in spring.**

▲ **The days are hot and long in summer.**

 How is summer different from winter?

What causes the seasons?

Did you know that Earth moves around the Sun? The path Earth takes around the Sun is called its **orbit**. Earth takes about 365 days, or one year, to orbit the Sun.

We know there is day and night because Earth spins on its axis. The axis also is tilted. Earth always tilts in the same direction on its axis.

Earth Tilts

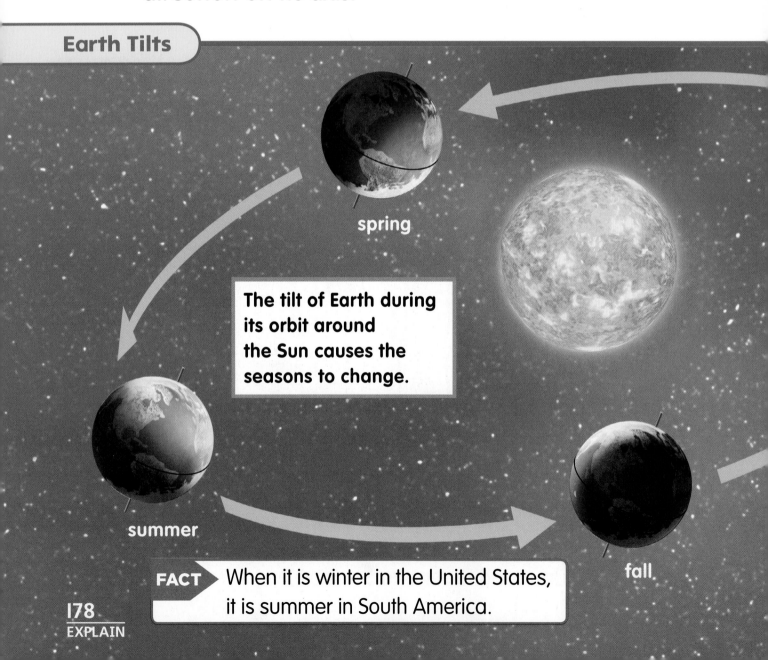

spring

The tilt of Earth during its orbit around the Sun causes the seasons to change.

summer

fall

FACT When it is winter in the United States, it is summer in South America.

As Earth moves around the Sun, the tilt of Earth causes the seasons. The part of Earth that tilts toward the Sun is warmer. The part of Earth that tilts away from the Sun is colder.

 What happens on Earth during one orbit around the Sun?

winter

Think, Talk, and Write

1. **Compare and Contrast.** How does the weather change in each season?

2. What causes summer and winter?

3. Write about how summer and winter are different.

Art Link

Use colored paper to make four collages. Make one for each season.

LOG ON ⓔ**-Review** Summaries and quizzes online at www.macmillanmh.com

Read a Diagram

Which season shows the top half of Earth tilted away from the Sun?

LOG ON *Science in Motion* Watch how Earth tilts at www.macmillanmh.com

Fun with the Seasons

Think about the seasons and the different things you do all year. Use the photographs to help you think about what you like to do.

 Write About It

Write a story to compare what you do in winter and in summer. Include details about how the seasons are alike and different.

Remember
Writing to compare tells how things are alike and different.

 e–Journal Write about it online at www.macmillanmh.com

 SI.2a. Identify similarities and differences between explanations received from others or in print and personal observations or understandings

How Much Sunlight?

We get more sunlight in the summer than we do in the winter. How many hours of sunlight do we get in each season? Use this chart to find out.

Hours of sunlight in one day

summer	$14\frac{1}{2}$ hours
fall	$11\frac{1}{2}$ hours
winter	10 hours
spring	12 hours

Put in Order

Put the seasons in order from least to most hours of sunlight. Make a new chart to show this.

Remember

Look at the whole numbers first to put numbers in order.

The Moon and Stars

Look and Wonder

The Moon is bright in the night sky. Where does the Moon's light come from?

PS-1.1 (a,c). Describe patterns of daily, monthly, and seasonal changes in their environment.

How do we see the Moon at night?

What to Do

1. Use a white ball as the Moon. Turn out the room lights. Is it easy to see the Moon?

flashlight

2. **Make a Model.** Shine a flashlight on the Moon. The flashlight is the Sun. Is the Moon easier to see now? Why?

white ball

3. **Draw Conclusions.** Where does the Moon's light come from?

Explore More

4. **Investigate.** What if the Moon were a different color? How would that affect the brightness of the Moon? Make a model to find out.

Step **2**

 S3.2a. State, orally and in writing, any inferences or generalizations indicated by the data collected

Why can we see the Moon from Earth?

The Moon does not shine the way the Sun does. The Moon is made of rock! We see the Moon because light from the Sun shines on the Moon.

Look at the picture below. Point to where it is night on Earth. Then point to the part of the Moon that is lit by the Sun. You sometimes see this part of the Moon at night.

How the Moon Moves

Sun

The Sun's light shines on the Moon.

Moon

Read a Diagram

When can we see the most light on the Moon?

The Moon does not just stay still in the night sky. The Moon moves in a path around Earth. It takes the Moon about a month to make one orbit around Earth. The Moon's path around Earth repeats again and again.

 Why can we see the Moon?

▲ **The Moon has a light color because it is covered in dust.**

Earth

Why does the Moon seem to change shape?

From Earth the Moon looks as if it is changing shape. The Moon does not really change shape. Our view of the Moon changes as the Moon moves during one month.

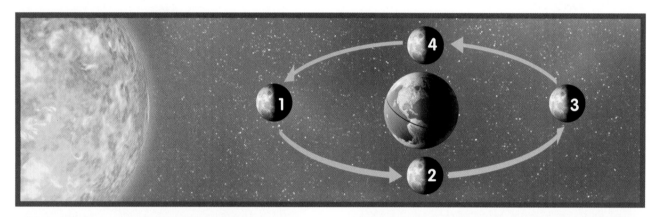

New Moon

When the Moon is between Earth and the Sun, we can not see the Sun's light shining on the Moon. It looks as if there is no Moon at all!

First Quarter Moon

After a week the Moon looks like this. It is called the First Quarter Moon. The Moon has completed $\frac{1}{4}$ of its orbit around Earth.

◀ **The Moon is Earth's closest neighbor in space.**

On different nights we see different amounts of sunlight shining on the Moon. Each shape of the Moon we see during one month is called a **phase**. The phases appear in the same order every month. The phases repeat each month.

✔ **What happens as the Moon orbits Earth?**

Full Moon

The Moon moves to a new place by the next week. We can see all of the Moon's lit side. This phase is called the Full Moon.

Last Quarter Moon

By the third week, the Moon is $\frac{3}{4}$ of its way around Earth. It is called the Last Quarter Moon.

FACT ▶ The Moon can sometimes be seen during the day.

What are stars?

A **star** is an object in space made of hot, glowing gases. The gases give off heat and light. Some stars are very bright. Stars can be different colors and sizes.

Some stars make patterns in the sky. Stars seem to move across the sky during one night.

Quick Lab

Observe the night sky. Collect data about the stars you see. Communicate what you see to your class.

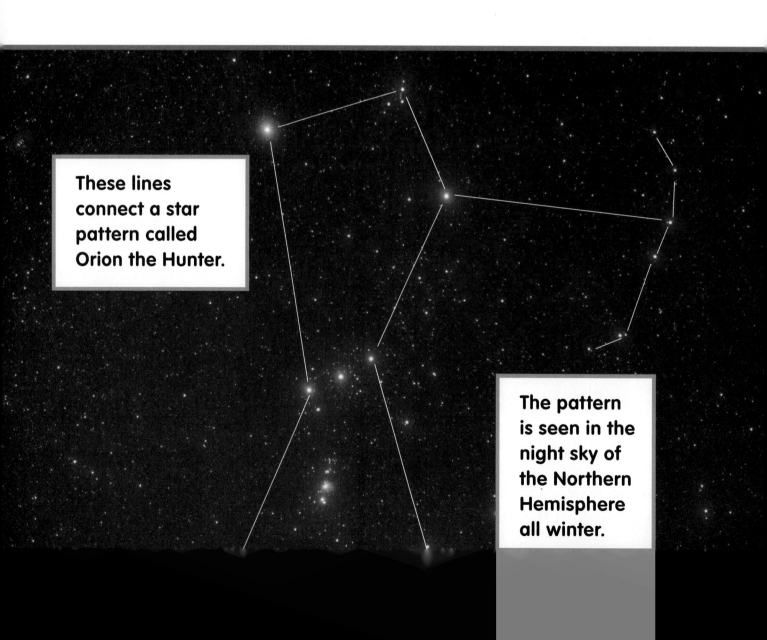

These lines connect a star pattern called Orion the Hunter.

The pattern is seen in the night sky of the Northern Hemisphere all winter.

From Earth, stars look like tiny points of light. They look tiny because they are far away.

There is one star that is close to Earth. That star is the Sun! The Sun is an average size star. It looks large to us because it is close to Earth.

 How are stars different from each other?

▲ **The Sun lights up the sky during the day. We can not see other stars in the sky until night.**

Think, Talk, and Write

1. **Predict.** What do you think will happen a week after a New Moon?

2. What star is closest to Earth?

3. Draw and write about how the Moon seems to change during one month.

Art Link*

Draw a pattern of stars on paper. Connect the stars. Give your star pattern a name.

LOG ON e-Review Summaries and quizzes online at www.macmillanmh.com

You need

calendar

markers

How does the Moon seem to change during one month?

Find out how the Moon seems to change shape each week.

What to Do

1 Observe. Look outside tonight. Find the Moon in the night sky.

2 Record Data. Draw what the Moon looks like on today's date on the calendar.

3 Repeat steps 1 and 2 each night for a month.

④ When did you see a full moon during the month? When did you see a new moon?

⑤ **Draw Conclusions.** What do your drawings tell you about the phases of the Moon?

Investigate More

Predict. How would the Moon look in the sky during the next month? Test your idea. Compare it to the calendar for this month.

▼ These photos show how the Moon seems to change during one month.

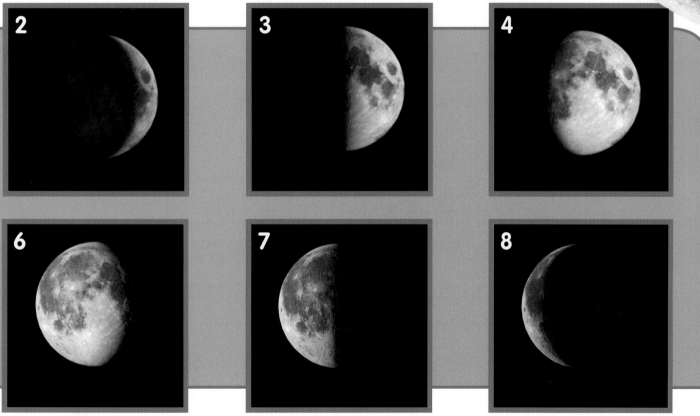

 M2.Ib. Explain verbally, graphically, or in writing patterns and relationships observed in the physical and living environment

Our Moving Earth

Our planet Earth is always moving. Every day it spins. It takes all day and all night for Earth to make one full turn.

When Earth has turned part of
the way around, we no longer see
the Sun. Now we see the Moon
and stars shining in the night sky.

spring

summer

Every day Earth also moves
farther on its trip around the
Sun. The whole trip around
the Sun takes a year.

fall

winter

Along the way Earth has four seasons. When the year is over, the trip around the Sun begins again!

Vocabulary

Use each word once for items 1–4.

1. The Moon's changing shapes are called _____.
   PS-1.1 (a)

2. We have day and night because Earth _____ once every 24 hours.
   PS-1.1 (a, b)

3. Every year Earth makes one _____ around the Sun.
   PS-1.1 (a, b)

4. This bright, hot _____ is also known as our Sun.
   PS-1.1 (c)

orbit

phases

rotates

star

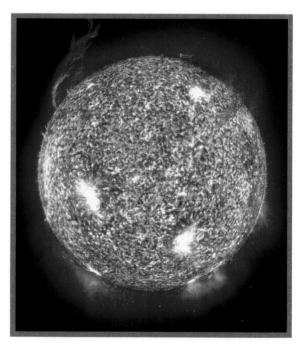

Answer the questions below.

5. What season do you think this photo shows? Why?

PS-I.I (a)

6. Draw Conclusions. Describe how Earth and the Moon travel around the Sun. Use balls and a flashlight to help describe what happens.

PS-I.I (a)

7. Compare and Contrast. What makes day and night?

PS-I.I (a)

8. Where does the Moon's light come from?

PS-I.I (a)

9. What can we see in the night sky?

PS-I

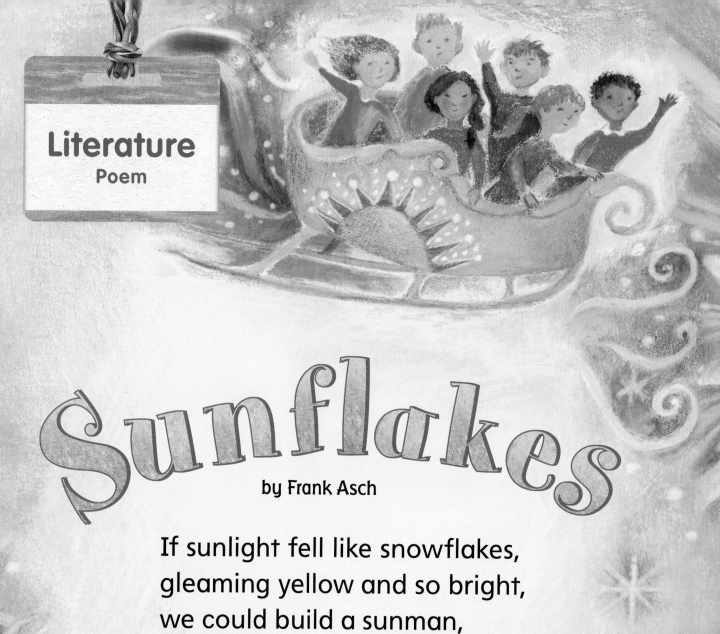

Sunflakes

by Frank Asch

If sunlight fell like snowflakes,
gleaming yellow and so bright,
we could build a sunman,
we could have a sunball fight,
we could watch the sunflakes
drifting in the sky.

We could go sleighing
in the middle of July
through sundrifts and sunbanks,
we could ride a sunmobile,
and we could touch sunflakes.
I wonder how they'd feel.

Talk About It

What do you think
sunflakes would look like?

Careers in Science

Gemologist

Have you seen people wearing rings or earrings with colorful stones in them? Many of these stones are called gems. Gemologists are scientists who study gems.

Gems are hard and rare minerals that are known for their beauty. Sapphires, emeralds, and diamonds are some gems.

The job of a gemologist is to identify a gem and to find out its quality and value. Gemologists use special tools to identify gems and see if they have cracks in them.

gemologist

More Careers to Think About

jewelry designer

volcanologist

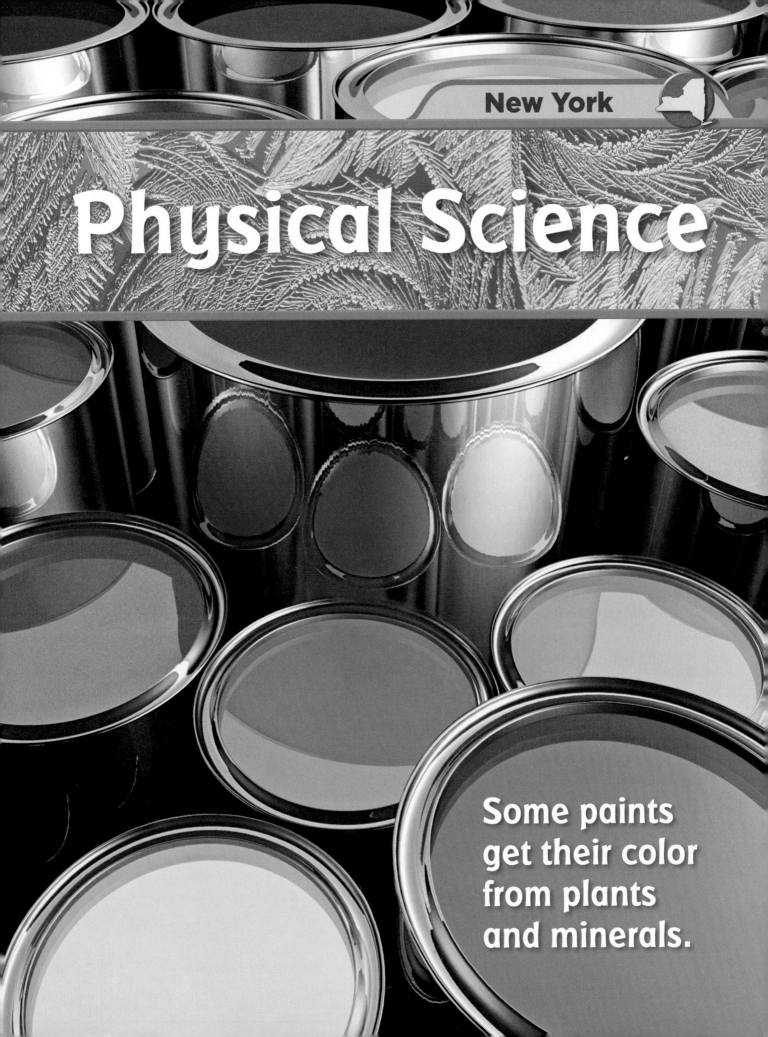

Physical Science

Some paints get their color from plants and minerals.

National Baseball Hall of Fame

National Baseball
Hall of Fame and Museum

a batter after
hitting a baseball

Playing with History

Did you know that The National Baseball Hall of Fame and Museum is in New York? Pictures and souvenirs in the museum tell the history of baseball. People have been playing baseball for over one hundred years.

Bats and Balls

Every push or pull is a force. A pitcher's throw is a force. The throw puts the ball in motion. Some pitchers can throw a baseball faster than a car can move!

The swing of a player's bat is also a force. The push from the bat changes the direction of the ball. The more force the player uses, the farther the ball will travel.

Think, Talk, and Write

Critical Thinking How are forces are used in baseball?

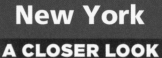

New York

A CLOSER LOOK

▶ **Main Idea**
Playing baseball uses forces.

▶ **Activity**

Compare Think of another activity or sport.

■ What are the push and pull forces in that activity? Compare your forces to the forces in baseball.

■ Share your answers with your classmates. Compare your lists.

PS-5.Ib. The position or direction of motion of an object can be changed by pushing or pulling.

203
NEW YORK

Montauk Point Lighthouse

a beam of light

New York's Oldest Lighthouse

Have you ever seen a lighthouse? There are many lighthouses in New York. Montauk Point is the oldest lighthouse in the state. This lighthouse was built in the 1790s. It is still working today!

Lighting the Way

Light is one form of energy. The light from a lighthouse travels in a straight line. A lens makes the light a bright beam. The beam of light is used as a guide for boats and small planes.

Lighthouses help keep ships safe in the dark. The light lets ships know how close they are getting to big rocks and shallow water near the shore.

Think, Talk, and Write

Critical Thinking What are some other ways that light is helpful?

► **Main Idea**

Light is a form of energy.

► **Activity**

Compare Think about a lighthouse and a street lamp. How are they alike? How are they different?

■ Write your answers on a poster with two columns. Label one column *Alike* and label the other column *Different.*

■ Compare your poster with your classmates.

PS-4.1a. Energy exists in various forms: heat, electric, sound, chemical, mechanical, light.

CHAPTER 6

Looking at Matter

The **Big Idea** How can we describe matter?

Key Vocabulary

mass the amount of matter in an object

(page 210)

solid matter that has a shape of its own

(page 218)

liquid matter that takes the shape of the container it is in

(page 226)

gas matter that spreads to fill the space it is in (page 228)

PS-3. Matter is made up of particles whose properties determine the observable characteristics of matter and its reactivity.

Describing Matter

hot air balloons in Aspen, Colorado

Look and Wonder

How are the things you see in this picture alike and different?

 PS-3.I (a,b,c,f). Observe and describe properties of materials, using appropriate tools.

How can you describe objects?

You need

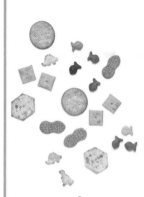

crackers

What to Do

1. **Observe.** Look at each cracker. Think about the different ways you can describe the crackers. What words can help you describe each one?

2. **Record Data.** Make a chart like the one shown. Write your observations on your chart.

3. **Classify.** Use your chart to help you sort the crackers.

Explore More

4. How else can you sort the crackers?

	texture	shape	size	color

S3.Ia. Accurately transfer data from a science journal or notes to appropriate graphic organizer

Vocabulary

matter

mass

property

What is matter?

Matter is anything that takes up space and has mass. **Mass** is the amount of matter in an object. The water that you drink is matter. The air you breathe is matter. Matter can be natural or made by people. We use matter every day.

Using Matter

Read a Photo

How is this boy using matter?

Different objects have different amounts of mass. A truck has a lot of mass. A pencil has a little mass. Does a book have more mass than a flower? Yes! A book feels heavier if you try to pick it up. We can use a balance to measure and compare mass.

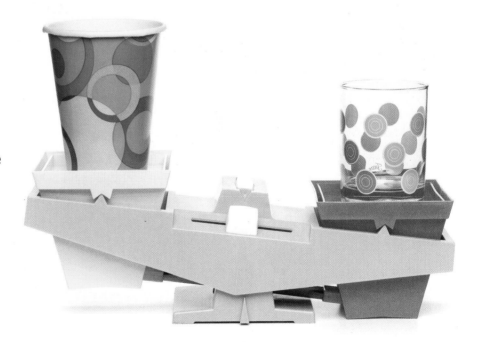

The larger shoe has more mass than the smaller shoe. ▶

Sometimes a smaller object can have more mass than a larger object. ▶

 What are some examples of matter found in your desk?

How can you describe matter?

You can describe matter by talking about its properties. A **property** is how matter looks, feels, smells, tastes, or sounds. Matter can feel smooth, rough, soft, or hard. Matter can be thick or thin. Matter can be living or nonliving.

Quick Lab

Investigate what sinks and what floats in water.

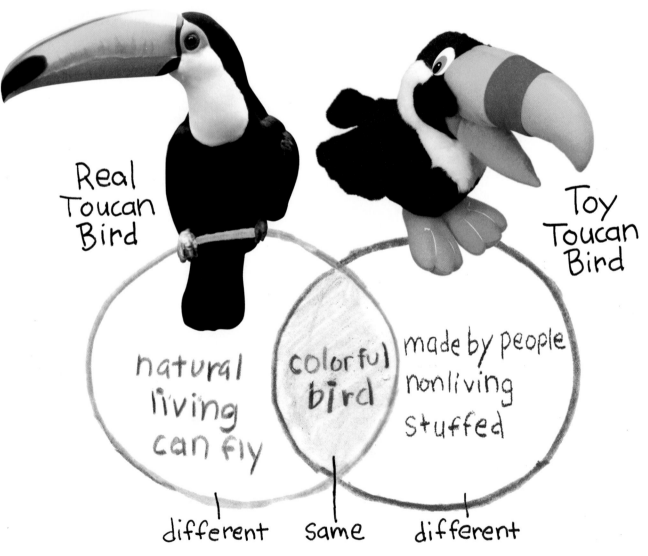

Real Toucan Bird

Toy Toucan Bird

natural living can fly

colorful bird

made by people nonliving stuffed

different   same   different

There are many ways to talk about matter. Matter can be solid, liquid, or gas.

 What are the properties of the things in the room around you?

▲ This mustard is thick and gooey.

Some balls float and others sink in water. ▶

Think, Talk, and Write

1. **Compare and Contrast.** Choose two objects. Make a list to compare their properties.

2. What is matter?

3. Write about which has more mass, a cotton ball or a baseball.

Art Link

Use different types of matter to make a collage.

LOG ON e-**Review** Summaries and quizzes online at www.macmillanmh.com

Focus on Skills

Inquiry Skill: Record Data

When you **record data**, you write down what you observe.

▶ Learn It

Joanie talked to each of her classmates about what they had for lunch. She made a tally chart to help her count the kinds of foods they ate. She recorded what was a liquid and what was a solid.

Then she made a bar graph from her results. A bar graph is a good way to compare data in different groups.

Our Lunch

| liquid | IIII |
| solid | HHt III |

Our Lunch

number of solids and liquids
0 1 2 3 4 5 6 7 8 9

▶ Try It

Look at this picture. Some things are natural and some are made by people. Make a tally chart to show how many of each thing you see. Then display your data in a bar graph.

1. How many things in the picture were made by people?

2. What kind of chart can help you record your data?

🖍 **3. Write About It.** How can a bar graph help you compare data?

 M2.1a. Explain verbally, graphically, or in writing the reasoning used to develop mathematical conclusions

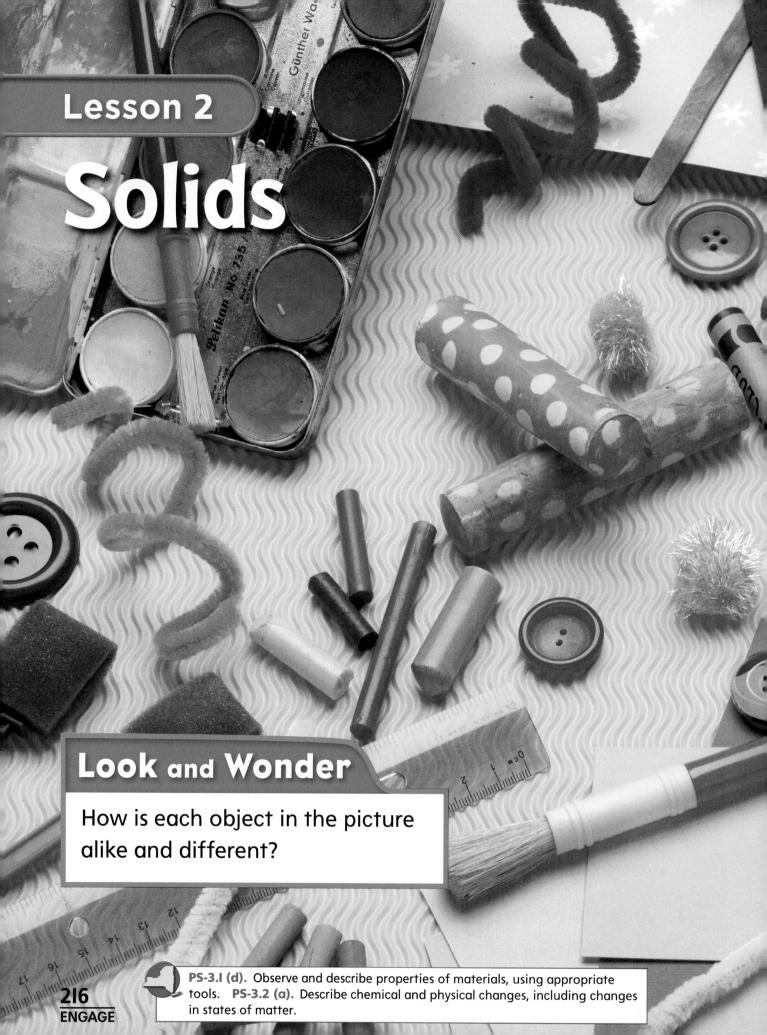

Look and Wonder

How is each object in the picture alike and different?

PS-3.1 (d). Observe and describe properties of materials, using appropriate tools. PS-3.2 (a). Describe chemical and physical changes, including changes in states of matter.

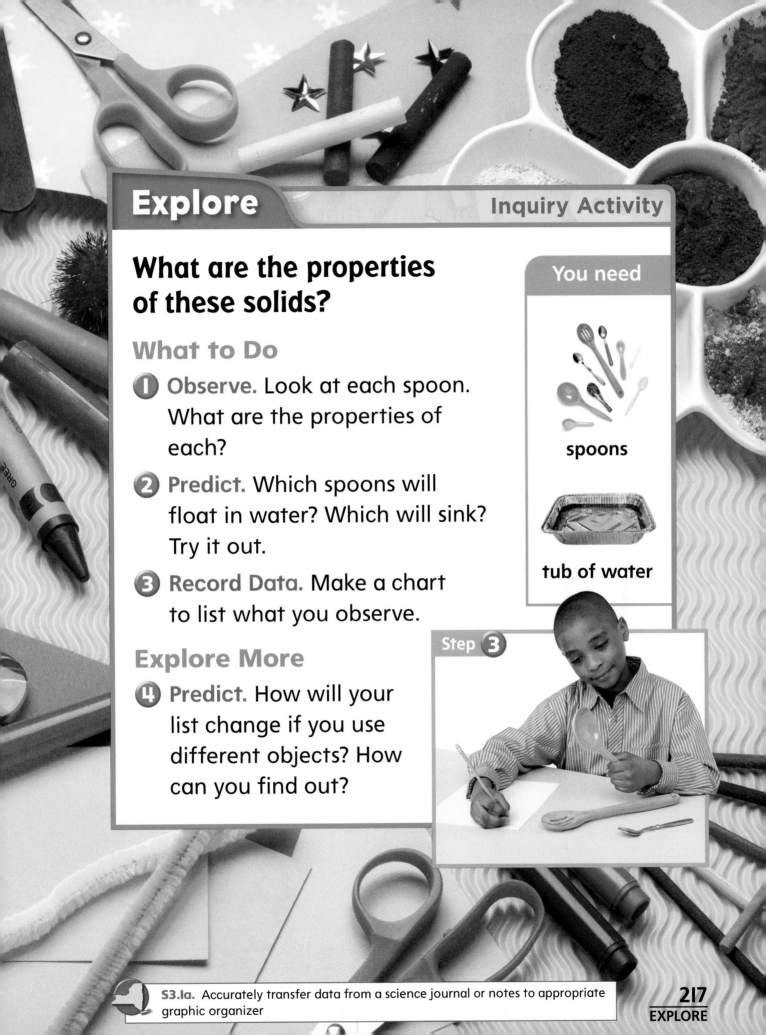

Explore

What are the properties of these solids?

What to Do

① Observe. Look at each spoon. What are the properties of each?

② Predict. Which spoons will float in water? Which will sink? Try it out.

③ Record Data. Make a chart to list what you observe.

Explore More

④ Predict. How will your list change if you use different objects? How can you find out?

You need

spoons

tub of water

Step **③**

S3.Ia. Accurately transfer data from a science journal or notes to appropriate graphic organizer

217
EXPLORE

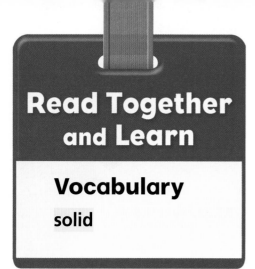
What is a solid?

What kind of matter do you see around you? A **solid** is a kind of matter that has a shape of its own. Like all matter, solids have properties. Some solids bend. Others tear. Some solids float in water. Other solids sink.

Some Properties of Solids

rock
- **hard**
- **speckled**
- **jagged**

glass
- **smooth**
- **breakable**
- **clear**

yarn
- **soft**
- **colorful**
- **long and thin**

FACT Not all solids are hard.

Solids are made of different materials. Some metals, woods, and plastics are hard. Materials can be smooth or rough when you touch them. The chart below shows the properties of some solids.

 What are some properties of solids?

toy

- blue
- pointy
- plastic

sea sponge

- yellow
- soft
- scratchy

clay

- sticky
- bendable
- firm

How can we measure solids?

We can use tools to measure solids. A ruler tells how long, wide, or high a solid is. Some rulers measure length in a unit called a centimeter. Other rulers measure in a unit called an inch. Many rulers give both measurements.

A balance tells how much mass something has. You can measure the same object in different ways. You can measure the mass and the length of a piece of chalk.

Quick Lab

Measure the mass of things in your classroom with a balance.

Read a Photo

What will happen to the balance if you add one more pencil to the left side?

LOG ON *Science in Motion* See how a balance measures matter at **www.macmillanmh.com**

Measuring Solids

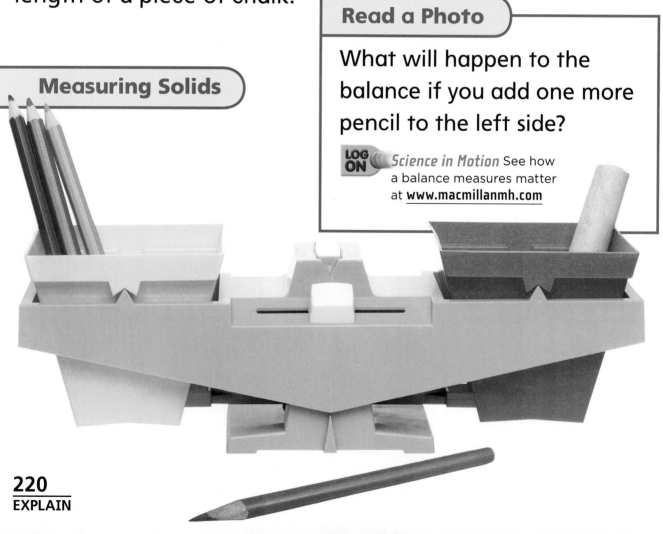

▶ The chalk is 10 centimeters long, or about 4 inches.

▶ Measure the distance around the chalk with string.

▶ Then measure the string with a ruler.

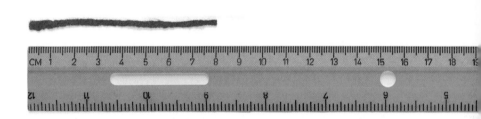

 What tools can we use to measure solids?

Think, Talk, and Write

1. **Summarize.** What are some properties of solids?

2. What are some examples of solid matter?

3. Write about a solid that you use every day.

Art Link

Find solids around the classroom. Make a piece of art showing some of their properties.

LOG ON e-Review Summaries and quizzes online at **www.macmillanmh.com**

Natural or Made by People?

This chair is made of wood. Wood is a natural product. It comes from trees. People cut down the trees. Then they shape the wood with tools to make the chair.

Wood can be painted or stained. Under the paint, the wood is still its original color.

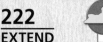 **SI.2a.** Identify similarities and differences between explanations received from others or in print and personal observations or understandings

This chair is made of plastic. Plastic is made by people. People combine chemicals to create plastic. Then they shape it in molds.

There are many different kinds of plastic. Plastic can be hard or bendable. People can also add a color to the chemicals in plastic. The plastic then becomes that color.

Which solids in your classroom are natural? Which are made by people?

Talk About It

Summarize. What is the difference between natural solids and solids made by people?

AMERICAN
MUSEUM ö
NATURAL
HISTORY

Liquids and Gases

Look and Wonder

Which glass is holding the most liquid?
Why do you think so?

PS-3.I (d). Observe and describe properties of materials, using appropriate tools. **PS-3.2 (a).** Describe chemical and physical changes, including changes in states of matter.

What happens to water in different shaped containers?

What to Do

1 Put containers on a tray. Measure one cup of water with the measuring cup. Pour the water into the first container. Mark where the water stops.

2 **Predict.** How high will the same amount of water be in the other containers?

3 Pour one cup of water into the next container. Mark where the water stops. Repeat for each container.

4 **Draw Conclusions.** Were your predictions correct? Explain.

Explore More

5 **Infer.** Would the activity change if you used juice instead of water? Why or why not?

You need

measuring cup

containers

tray

Step **3**

Read Together and Learn

Vocabulary

liquid
volume
gas

What is a liquid?

A **liquid** is a kind of matter that takes the shape of the container it is in. Without a container, liquids flow and have no shape.

All liquids have mass. Liquids can be thin like milk or thick like honey.

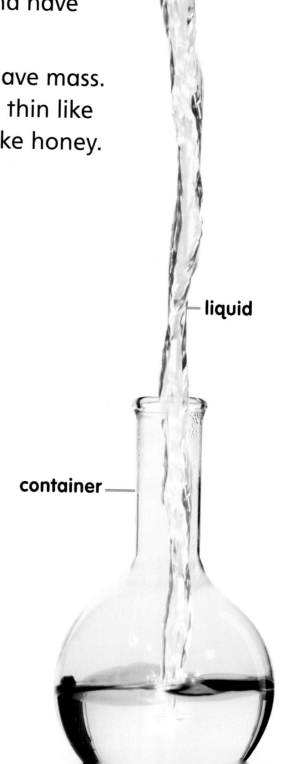

liquid

container

Even in nature, liquid takes the shape of the space it is in. This waterfall flows and fills the shape of the lake.

The amount of space something takes up is called **volume**. You can measure the volume of a liquid with a measuring cup. Liquids are measured in milliliters or ounces.

The measuring cups in the picture can hold the same amount. One cup is holding a greater volume of liquid than the other.

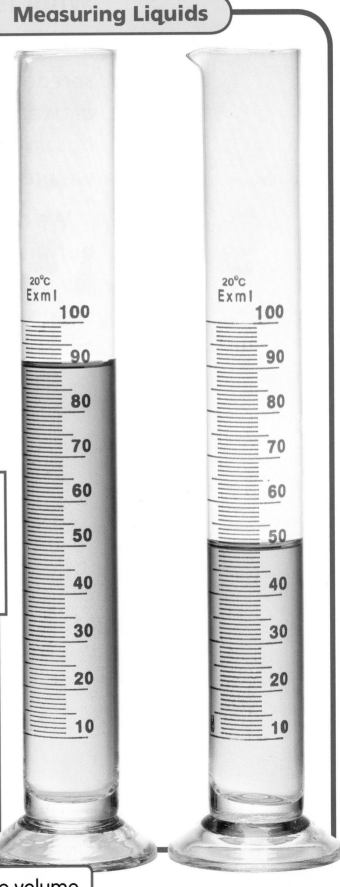

Read a Photo

How many milliliters of liquid are in each container?

✓ What are some properties of liquids?

FACT Solids and gases also have volume.

What is a gas?

A **gas** is a kind of matter that spreads to fill the space it is in. The air we breathe is made of many gases. Oxygen is one of the gases we breathe.

We cannot see the gases in the air, but they are all around us. We can tell gases are there when they fill a balloon or a beach ball. We can feel air moving on a windy day.

Gases have no shape of their own.

Remember that anything that takes up space is matter. All matter has mass. How can you tell that gas has mass? Look at the picture.

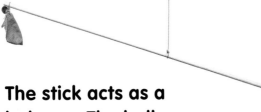

The stick acts as a balance. The balloon filled with air has more mass than the one without air.

Quick Lab

Fill containers with different kinds of matter. Have a partner **classify** the matter as solid, liquid, or gas.

 What are some properties of a gas?

Think, Talk, and Write

1. **Classify.** List the items in your refrigerator. Sort them as solid, liquid, or gas.

2. How is a gas different from a liquid?

3. Write a list of words that can be used to describe liquids. Share your list with a friend.

Health Link

Make a list of liquids that are good for you.

Fun with Water

This girl is having fun in the water! How do you enjoy water?

✏ Write About It

Think of times that you have had fun in water. Draw and write about what you did. Remember to add details to your story.

Remember

Details help your reader know what happened and how you felt.

 LOG ON ℮ **–Journal** Write about it online at **www.macmillanmh.com**

S3.la. Accurately transfer data from a science journal or notes to appropriate graphic organizer   **M2.lb** Explain verbally, graphically, or in writing patterns and relationships observed in the physical and living environment

Which Has More Volume?

Matt put juice in two measuring cups. What can you tell about the two containers of juice? Which has more volume?

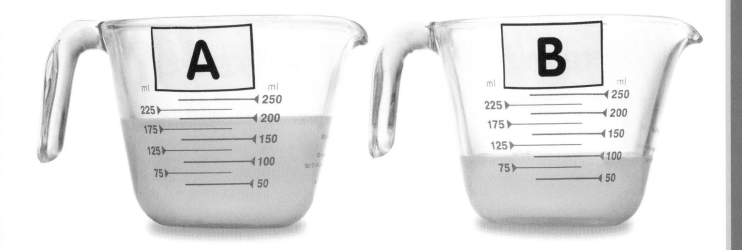

Write a Number Sentence

Cup A has 200 mL of juice. Cup B has 100 mL of juice. How many more mL are in Cup A?

Write a number sentence to show how you found the answer.

Remember

Think about which operation to choose.

MI.Ia. Use plus, minus, greater than, less than, equal to, multiplication, and division signs

Matter Changes

Look and Wonder

What matter is being changed here?

PS-3.1 (g). Observe and describe properties of materials, using appropriate tools. **PS-3.2 (a,b).** Describe chemical and physical changes, including changes in states of matter.

How can clay be changed?

What to Do

You need

modeling clay

① **Measure.** Find two pieces of clay that are the same mass. Use a balance to show they are equal.

② **Squeeze** and shape one piece of clay into a ball. Describe its properties.

balance

③ **Predict.** Do you think the mass of the clay changed after it was made into a ball? Place it back on the balance to find out.

plastic knife

④ ⚠ **Be Careful!** Cut the clay ball into two halves with a plastic knife. Make the two pieces into two figures.

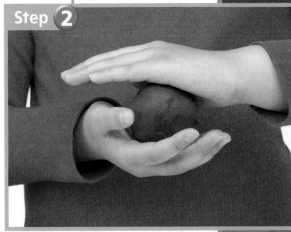

Step ②

⑤ **Draw Conclusions.** How did you change the clay?

Explore More

⑥ **Investigate.** What other ways can you change clay? Will the mass change?

What are physical changes?

Matter can change in different ways. You can change the size or shape of matter. This is called a **physical change**.

When you cut, bend, fold, or tear matter, you cause a physical change. You can change the shape or size of paper by cutting or folding it. It is still paper. Its properties are the same.

◀ **Folding and writing on paper are physical changes.**

When you only change the shape of matter, its mass stays the same. ▼

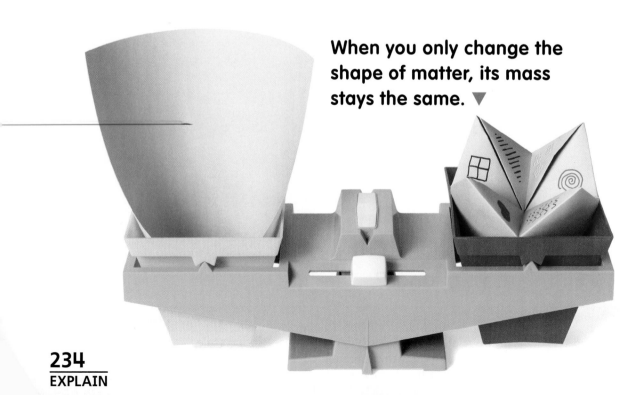

Sometimes the temperature of matter changes. On a cold day, water can change to ice. This is a physical change.

Wetting and drying can be physical changes, too. Wet mud looks and feels different from dry mud.

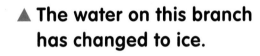
▲ The water on this branch has changed to ice.

✔ What is a physical change you could make to juice?

The color of dry mud is different from wet mud. Mud feels squishy when it is wet, and hard when it is dry.

What are chemical changes?

Sometimes the properties of matter can change. This is called a **chemical change**. When matter goes through a chemical change, sometimes it is not easy to change it back. It becomes a new kind of matter with different properties.

When you burn paper, you can not change it back. Seeing light and feeling heat are clues that a chemical change may be happening. All matter does not change in the same way.

Quick Lab

Observe a slice of apple. Infer what causes the apple to go through a chemical change.

Chemical Changes		
Before	**After**	**Cause**
		Heat causes the matchstick to burn. The properties of the matchstick have changed.
		Water and air can cause metal to rust. Rust is a chemical change that happens slowly.
		Water and air do not change the properties of plastic.

Read a Chart

How did the metal nail change?

Heat causes the egg to go through a chemical change that you can see and smell.

✓ How can you tell if a chemical change has happened?

Think, Talk, and Write

1. **Problem and Solution.** Describe how you could keep a bicycle from rusting.

2. What are three examples of physical changes?

3. What happens to a banana peel over time? Write about it.

Math Link

Does the mass of an object change when you fold the object? How could you find out?

LOG ON ℮-Review Summaries and quizzes online at **www.macmillanmh.com**

Inquiry Skill: Communicate

You **communicate** when you draw, write, or share your ideas with others.

▶ **Learn It**

Joanne changed a ball of clay. She wrote a list to show others how she changed it.

Changing Clay

1. I rolled the clay.
2. I pinched the clay.
3. I squeezed the clay.
4. I poked the clay.

▶ **Try It**

How many ways can you change a piece of paper?

I. Use a chart like Joanne's to communicate how you changed the paper.

2. Share your chart with a classmate.

3. Write About It. Tell how your charts are alike and how they are different.

 SI.2a. Identify similarities and differences between explanations received from others or in print and personal observations or understandings

239
EXTEND

Changes of State

Kilauea Volcano, Hawaii

Look and Wonder

Volcanoes are so hot that rocks can melt and flow like a liquid. How else can heat change things?

PS-3.1 (g). Observe and describe properties of materials, using appropriate tools. **PS-3.2 (a,b).** Describe chemical and physical changes, including changes in states of matter.

How can heat change matter?

What to Do

① Predict. What do you think will happen to butter and chocolate in sunlight?

② Observe. Place the butter and chocolate on two plates. Draw how they look.

③ Predict. How will the Sun's heat change each thing? Find a sunny spot. Leave the plates in the sunlight.

④ Communicate. What happens to each thing after one hour? Draw how they look. Compare your pictures.

Explore More

⑤ Now try another item. How will it change?

You need

paper plates

butter

chocolate

Step **②**

 SI.Ia. Observe and discuss objects and events and record observations
S2.3a. Use appropriate "inquiry and process skills" to collect data

241
EXPLORE

Vocabulary

evaporate

condense

How can heating change matter?

Have you ever left a bar of chocolate in your pocket in summer? When you reached in to get it, chances are it was melting.

Melting means changing from a solid to a liquid. Some solids, like gold and glass, will only melt when they are very hot. Other solids, like ice and butter, melt at much lower temperatures.

◀ When gold melts, you can pour it into molds. As the gold cools, it will harden.

▼ **Solid ice cubes melt when left at room temperature.**

Water can change to a gas when it is heated. **Evaporate** means to change from liquid to gas and go into the air.

If enough heat is added to water, it will boil. When water boils, you can see bubbles. The bubbles show that the water is changing to a gas called water vapor. We can not see water vapor.

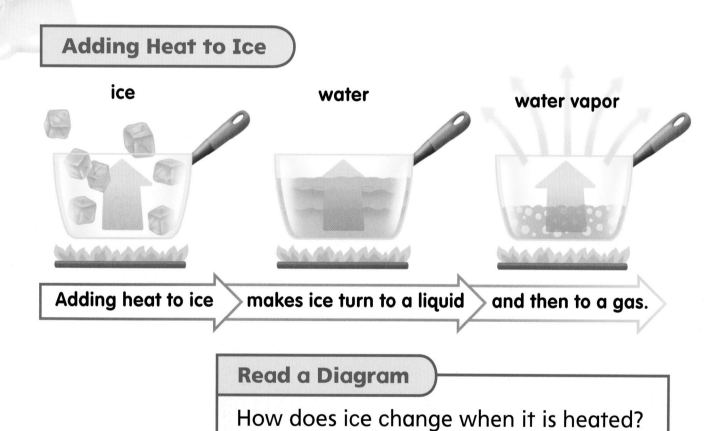

Adding Heat to Ice

ice   water   water vapor

Adding heat to ice > makes ice turn to a liquid > and then to a gas.

Read a Diagram

How does ice change when it is heated?

LOG ON *Science in Motion* Watch what happens when heat melts ice at **www.macmillanmh.com**

 How can heat change solids?

How can cooling change matter?

Matter can also change by cooling, or taking away heat. Gases condense when they are cooled. **Condense** means to change from a gas to a liquid.

Water vapor in the air condenses when it touches cool objects. This is why you see small drops of water on the outside of a cold glass.

▲ **Water vapor condenses on the outside of a bottle.**

FACT ▶ Water that has condensed on a window comes from air inside the room.

When liquids cool, they can freeze, or become solid. Wax and some other liquids will freeze at room temperature. Other liquids, like water, need to be much colder to freeze.

 How does water change when it is cooled?

After a candle burns, the wax will cool and become solid. ▶

Think, Talk, and Write

1. **Predict.** What will happen to a puddle of water on a sunny day?

2. What happens when water vapor condenses?

3. Draw and write about how you could change water from a solid to a liquid and back to a solid again.

Math Link

Do you think the mass of ice changes when it melts? How could you find out?

Colorful Creations

There are all kinds of colors inside your crayon box.
How were those crayons made?

Most crayons are made of wax. This man adds special dye to a tub of wax to give the wax color.

The colored wax is melted into a liquid. Then a worker pours this hot wax into a mold.

Inside the mold there are hundreds of holes shaped like crayons. The wax fills each hole. Then the mold is cooled with cold water.

  S3.Ia. Accurately transfer data from a science journal or notes to appropriate graphic organizer

This machine packs the crayons into boxes.

This woman checks the crayons by hand to make sure they are good.

Talk About It

Predict. What will happen if the mixture of wax is left out at room temperature?

AMERICAN MUSEUM ᴼꜰ NATURAL HISTORY

How Things Change

All around me, matter changes. Cutting is a physical change. Even though there are more pieces, this is still an apple. Physical changes do not change what something is.

All around me, matter changes. Batter cooks in the oven and becomes a muffin. This is a chemical change. The batter has new properties now.

All around me, matter changes. I can make a mixture of chocolate powder and milk. The chocolate milk stays mixed. It is a solution.

All around me, matter changes. I can freeze juice. When something freezes, it changes to a solid.

251

Vocabulary

Use each word once for items 1–6.

1. Everything that takes up space and has mass is called _____.
   PS-3.1 (a)

2. The amount of matter in something is called _____.
   PS-3.1 (a)

3. Water in the air can _____ or change into a liquid.
   PS-2.1 (c); PS 3.2 (b)

4. Matter that has a shape of its own is called a _____.
   PS-3.2 (a)

5. Matter that flows and takes the shape of the container it is in is called a _____.
   PS-3.2 (a)

6. After the snowman melts, the water will turn to a gas or _____.
   PS-2.1 (c); PS-3.2 (a,b)

condense

evaporate

liquid

mass

matter

solid

Answer the questions below.

7. **Communicate.** Which photo shows a physical change? Which shows a chemical change? What are some other examples of each kind of change?

PS-3.I (g); PS-3.2 (c)

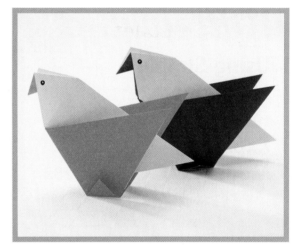

8. **Summarize.** What tools can you use to measure matter in different ways?

PS-3.I (b,d,e)

9. What type of matter has filled this balloon?

PS-3.2 (a)

10. How can we describe matter?

PS-3

How Things Move

The Big Idea

How do things move?

steam train in Silverton, Colorado

Key Vocabulary

motion a change in the position of an object (page 259)

friction a force that slows down moving things (page 269)

lever a simple machine made of a bar that turns around a point (page 276)

repel to push away or apart (page 286)

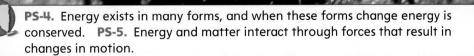

PS-4. Energy exists in many forms, and when these forms change energy is conserved. **PS-5.** Energy and matter interact through forces that result in changes in motion.

Position and Motion

Look and Wonder

Look at the dogs in this picture. How would you describe where they are? What words could you use?

PS-5.1 (a). Describe the effects of common forces (pushes and pulls) of objects, such as those caused by gravity, magnetism, and mechanical forces.

What words help us find things?

What to Do

1. Work with a partner. Pick an object in the classroom. Do not tell your partner what the object is.

2. **Communicate.** Describe where your object is. Give clues to your partner. Ask your partner to find the object.

3. Switch with your partner and try again.

4. **Draw Conclusions.** Which words in your description were most helpful to your partner?

Explore More

5. **Communicate.** Draw a picture and write directions to find an object in your picture. Then switch with a partner.

S3.4a. State, orally and in writing, any inferences or generalizations indicated by the data, with appropriate modifications of their original prediction/explanation

257
EXPLORE

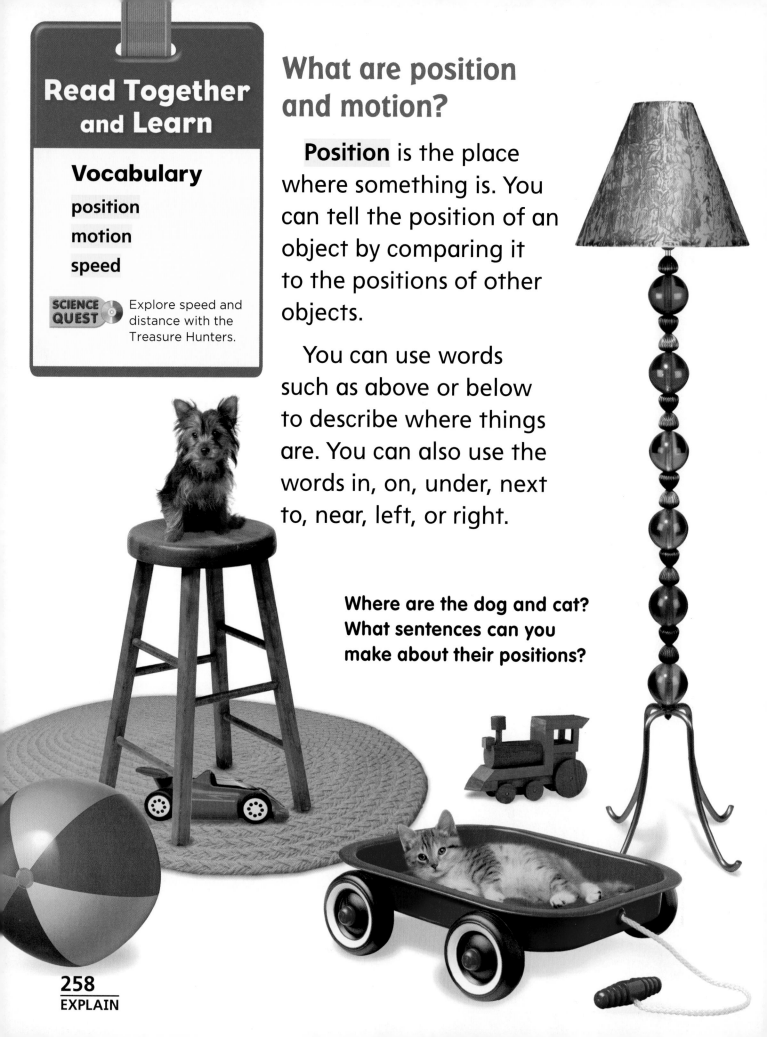

What are position and motion?

Position is the place where something is. You can tell the position of an object by comparing it to the positions of other objects.

You can use words such as above or below to describe where things are. You can also use the words in, on, under, next to, near, left, or right.

Where are the dog and cat? What sentences can you make about their positions?

When something moves, its position changes. **Motion** is a change in the position of an object. Some ways objects move are up, down, around, sideways, or zigzag. You can describe an object's motion by telling how its position changed.

✓ How can you describe where an object is and how it moves?

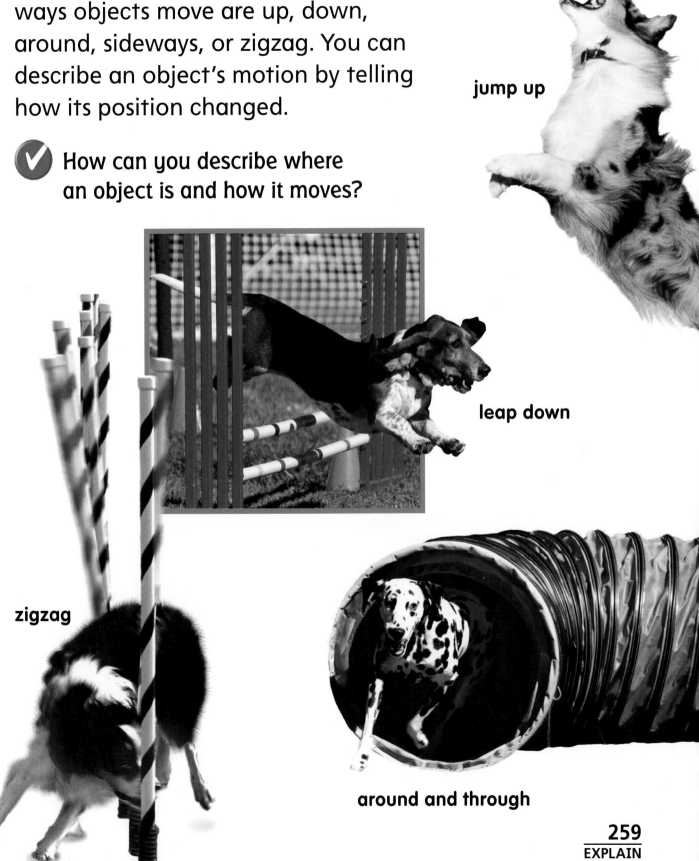

jump up

leap down

zigzag

around and through

What is speed?

Some things, such as snails, move slowly. Others, such as cheetahs, move quickly. **Speed** is how far something moves in a certain amount of time.

Quick Lab

Measure three meters in the classroom. Walk and then hop the distance. Record the time it took for each.

A cheetah's speed can be measured with a stopwatch and a tape measure. The fastest objects move farthest in a certain amount of time.

Animal Speed

animal

zebra

cheetah

lion

miles per hour

0 10 20 30 40 50 60 70

Read a Graph

Which animal is the fastest?

 What are some objects that move at high speeds?

Think, Talk, and Write

1. **Sequence.** You walk from your desk to your teacher's desk. Describe the order of objects you would pass as you move.

2. What are some words that you can use to describe motion?

3. Write about what speed is.

Social Studies Link

Make a map of your classroom. Draw yourself on the map and describe your position.

Inquiry Skill: Investigate

When you **investigate**, you make a plan and test it out.

▶ **Learn It**

Joe and Pat will run in a race. They want to find their speeds. They make a plan.

First, they measure 20 meters. They make a start and a finish line. Next, they measure the time it took them to run the distance.

Look at the chart. Who is faster?

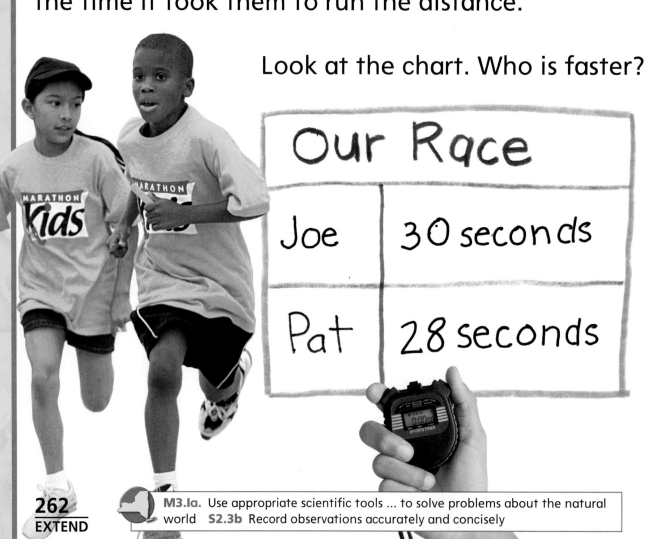

Our Race	
Joe	30 seconds
Pat	28 seconds

M3.la. Use appropriate scientific tools ... to solve problems about the natural world **S2.3b** Record observations accurately and concisely

▶ Try It

Which toy moves fastest? Make a plan to find out. Then test your plan.

I. Put tape on the floor to make a start line. Measure how far away your finish line will be. Mark it with tape.

masking tape

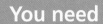

ruler

windup toys

stopwatch

2. Use a stopwatch to find out how long it took each toy to go the distance. Record the times.

3. Which toy was fastest?

Forces

Look and Wonder

How can you make something move?
How can you make it move farther?

 PS-4.1 (a). Describe a variety of forms of energy ... and the changes that occur in objects when they interact with those forms of energy. **PS-5.1 (b,c,d,f).** Describe the effects of common forces ... of objects, such as those caused by gravity, magnetism, and mechanical forces. **PS-5.2 (a).** Describe how forces can operate across distances.

How do you make things go farther and faster?

What to Do

1 Line up the car at a starting line. Push the car gently over the line.

2 Measure. How far did it go?

3 Do the activity again, but this time push the car harder. Observe what happens.

Explore More

4 Predict. What might happen if you pulled the car toward you with your hands? Would it go as far?

You need

toy car

masking tape

ruler

Step **2**

M3.Ia. Use appropriate scientific tools, such as metric rulers, spring scale, pan balance, graph paper, thermometers [Fahrenheit and Celsius], graduated cylinder to solve problems about the natural world

Vocabulary

force

gravity

friction

 SCIENCE QUEST Explore pushes and pulls with the Treasure Hunters.

What makes things move?

Objects can not start to move on their own. You have to use a push or a pull to put something in motion.

When you play soccer, you kick the ball to move it across the field. Your kick is a push. If you do not kick the ball, it will stay in the same place.

A stronger kick will make an object move farther.

A push or pull is called a **force**. If you push something, it will move away from you. If you pull it, it will move closer to you.

What is making the cart move?

A kick is a kind of push. Opening a drawer is a kind of pull. You can move different objects with different amounts of force.

 Why do we need forces?

Both groups are pulling the rope. Why does it not move?

What are some forces?

When you let go of a ball, it falls. **Gravity** is a force that pulls down on everything on Earth. When you jump in the air, gravity pulls you back down to the ground. Gravity pulls on objects through solids, liquids, and gases. The amount of force that pulls something down toward Earth is called its weight.

Why is the ball falling? What do you think will happen to the dog?

FACT All planets have gravity.

When you skate, you drag a rubber stopper on the ground to stop. The dragging causes friction. **Friction** is a force that slows down moving things. Friction happens when two things rub together.

There is usually more friction on rough surfaces than on smooth ones. It is usually harder to push or pull something on a rough surface than on a smooth surface.

✓ How are gravity and friction alike?

Quick Lab

Slide a wooden block on different slanted surfaces. **Compare** how friction affects the speed of the block.

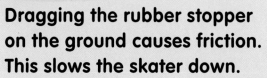

Dragging the rubber stopper on the ground causes friction. This slows the skater down.

The ball falls to the grass and rolls. Friction makes the ball slow down and stop. ▼

How can forces change motion?

You know that forces can change how things move. Forces can make things start moving, speed up, slow down, and stop. Forces can make things change direction, too. In softball, the players use forces to change the direction of the ball.

 Think about a sport that uses a ball. How does the ball change direction?

How a Ball Changes Direction

◄ The batter hits the ball with a push. It changes direction and flies toward the outfield.

The player in the outfield catches the ball and uses a force to stop its motion. He can also use a force to throw the ball to another player. ▶

Read a Diagram

What kind of forces do the players use?

LOG ON *Science in Motion* Watch forces work at **www.macmillanmh.com**

Think, Talk, and Write

1. **Cause and Effect.** What happens when you put more force on an object?

2. Why is it hard to push something on some surfaces?

3. Write a story about a day without gravity.

Social Studies Link

Learn about a sport played in another country. Describe the pushes and pulls in this sport.

LOG ON **e-Review** Summaries and quizzes online at **www.macmillanmh.com**

Meet Héctor Arce

Héctor Arce is a scientist at the American Museum of Natural History. Héctor studies how stars form. When gravity pulls together huge clouds of gas and dust, stars form. Gravity makes their centers so hot that they light up. This is why stars shine in our night sky.

Gravity is the force that keeps you on Earth. You may not be able to see gravity, but it is all around you. In fact, it is everywhere! There is gravity on planets, moons, and stars. How powerful is gravity? It is powerful enough to create a star!

Héctor Arce is an astrophysicist, a scientist who studies the planets, moons, and stars.

S3.Ia. Accurately transfer data from a science journal or notes to appropriate graphic organizer

Héctor uses a telescope like the one in this building to get a closer look at stars.

Talk About It
Cause and Effect.
How do stars form?

AMERICAN
MUSEUM

Using Simple Machines

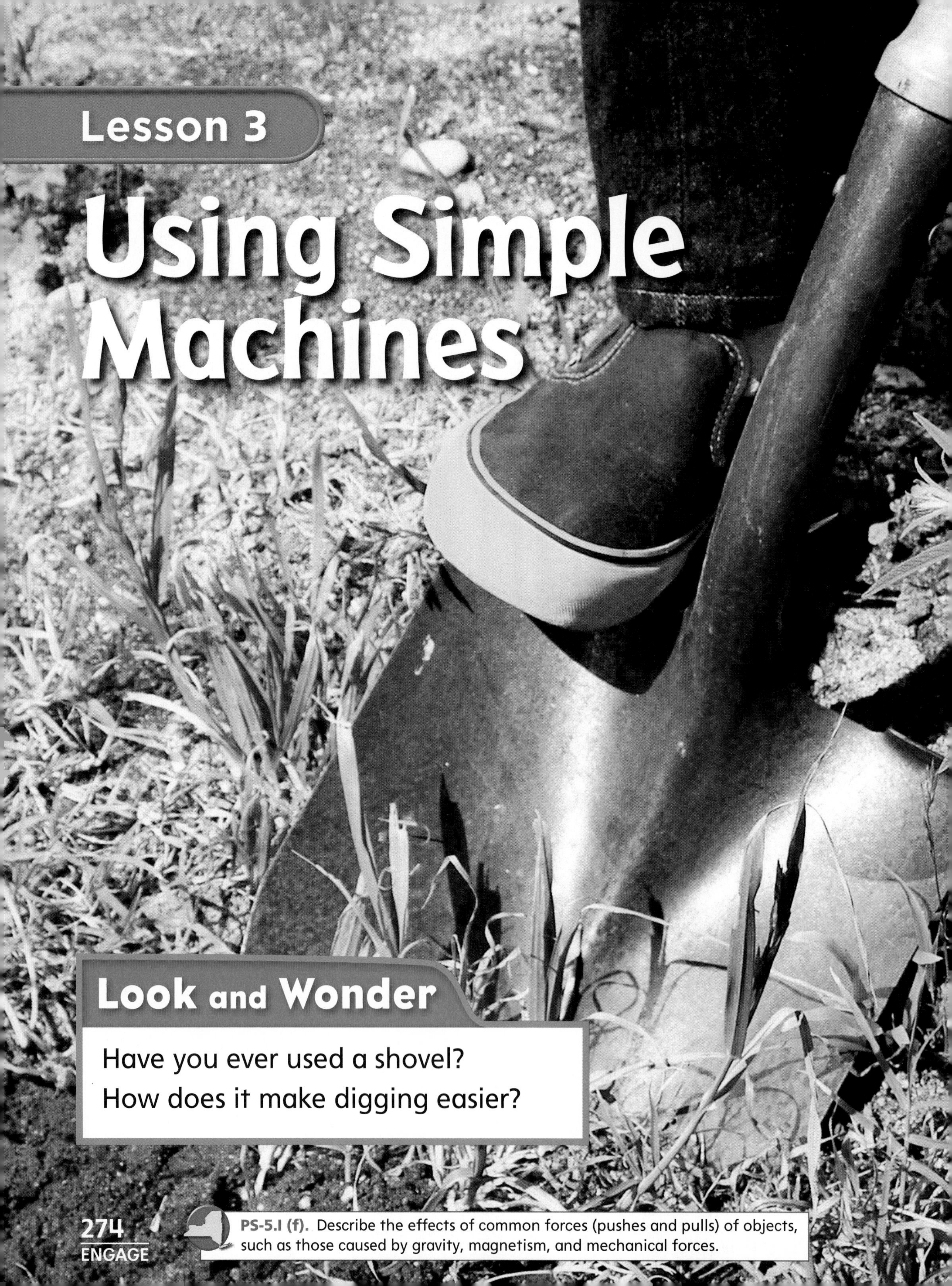

Look and Wonder

Have you ever used a shovel?
How does it make digging easier?

PS-5.I (f). Describe the effects of common forces (pushes and pulls) of objects, such as those caused by gravity, magnetism, and mechanical forces.

Which side will go up?

What to Do

1 Tape a marker to the middle of your desk.

2 Tape 10 pennies to the edge of one end of a ruler. Tape 5 pennies to the edge of the other end.

3 **Predict.** What will happen if you put the middle of the ruler on the marker? Which side will lift up? Try it. Was your prediction correct?

Explore More

4 Try to move the ruler so that 5 pennies can lift 10 pennies. Where did you need to move the ruler?

You need

marker

tape

ruler

15 pennies

Step **2**

SI.3a. Clearly express a tentative explanation or description which can be tested

What are levers and ramps?

A **simple machine** is a tool that changes the size or direction of a force. A simple machine can make work easier.

A **lever** is a bar that moves against an unmoving point. The unmoving point that a lever moves against is called a **fulcrum**. Shovels and seesaws are levers. When you push down on one side of the lever, the other side moves up.

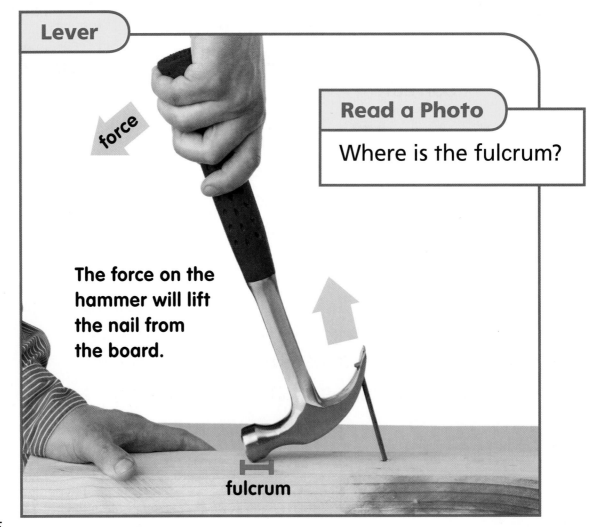

Lever

force

The force on the hammer will lift the nail from the board.

Read a Photo

Where is the fulcrum?

fulcrum

Pushing a heavy box up a ramp needs less force than lifting the box.

Another kind of simple machine is a ramp. A **ramp** is a surface that is straight and slanted. Ramps can be used to move an object from one place to another. Pushing something up a ramp is easier than lifting it. Less force is needed to move something on a long, low ramp than on a short, steep ramp.

 How do a lever and ramp make work easier?

What are other simple machines?

A bicycle uses a simple machine called a wheel and axle. A wheel and axle is made of a wheel and a bar, or axle. The bar is connected to the center of the wheel. When the wheel turns, the bar turns too.

A doorknob and a steering wheel use a wheel and axle. Each axle on a car or bus has two wheels attached.

Quick Lab

Investigate how to make a pulley. Use the pulley to lift a pail filled with blocks.

Where is the axle on this monster truck?

A pulley is also a simple machine. A pulley is made with a rope that moves around a wheel. When you attach a pulley to a object, you can change the direction of the force on the object. A pulley can help lift an object up high.

 When might it be helpful to use a pulley?

When you pull the rope down, the pig in the pail goes up to the pulley.

Think, Talk, and Write

1. **Summarize.** How can simple machines help you?

2. What are some kinds of simple machines?

3. Write about a simple machine used in your home.

Math Link

Make a tally chart of simple machines used at home and school.

LOG ON **e-Review** Summaries and quizzes online at **www.macmillanmh.com**

Slip and Slide

Have you ever walked on ice? It is smooth and slippery! Sometimes penguins slide on their bellies to move.

 Write About It

Explain why penguins can slide on the ice. Think about what you learned about forces. Make sure to explain why ice is slippery.

Remember
When you write to give information, you give facts.

LOG ON **e-Journal** Write about it online at **www.macmillanmh.com**

 S1.3a. Clearly express a tentative explanation or description which can be tested **S3.4a.** State, orally, and in writing, any inferences or generalizations indicated by the data, with appropriate modifications of their original prediction/explanation

How Far Did It Move?

These students are playing softball.
They want to know how far the ball moved.

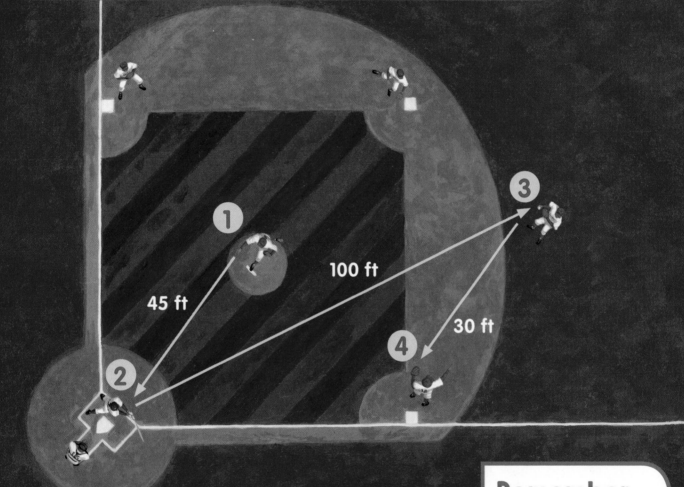

Add Measurements

Add the distances the ball moved. How far did it go? How many times did the ball change directions? Make up your own math problem about the softball game.

Remember

Add the 1s first. Then add the 10s. Then add the 100s.

 MI.Ia. Use plus, minus, greater than, less than, equal to, multiplication, and division signs

281
EXTEND

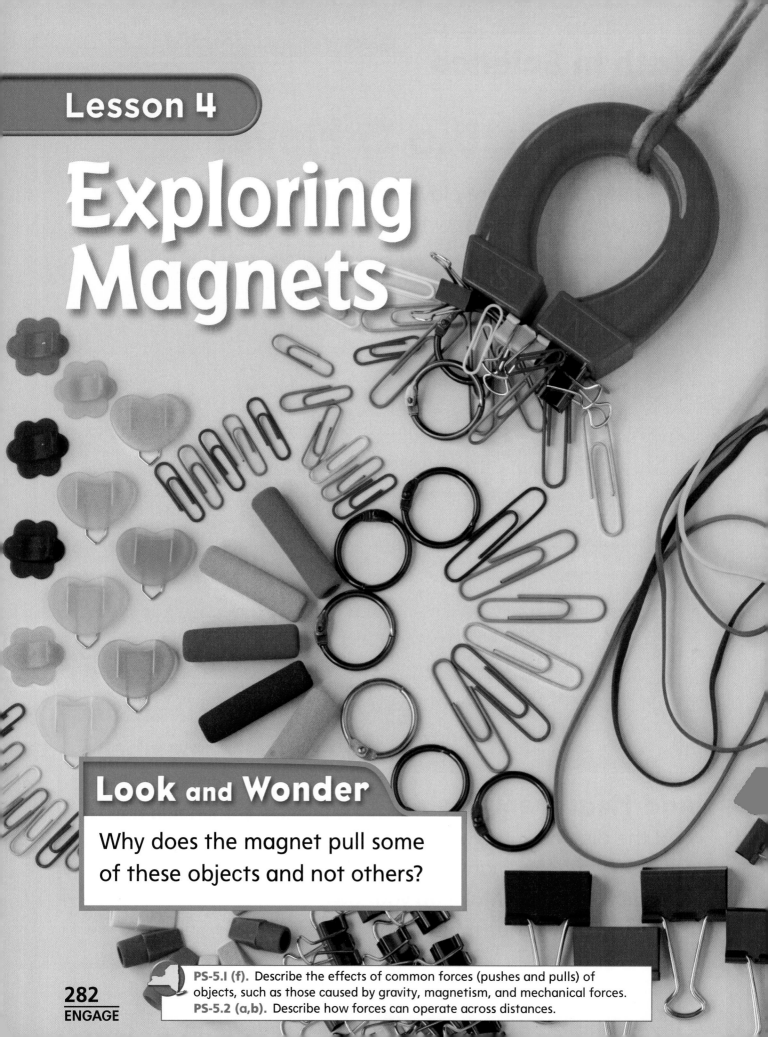

Exploring Magnets

Look and Wonder

Why does the magnet pull some of these objects and not others?

PS-5.I (f). Describe the effects of common forces (pushes and pulls) of objects, such as those caused by gravity, magnetism, and mechanical forces.
PS-5.2 (a,b). Describe how forces can operate across distances.

What can a magnet pick up?

What to Do

You need

small objects

1 **Predict.** Put the objects in a bag. Which objects will stick to a magnet?

2 Tie a string to a pencil. Tie a magnet to the end of the string.

3 Use the magnet to pull out objects from the bag.

paper bag

Step 3

string

pencil

Explore More

4 **Classify.** How are the things that stick to the magnet alike?

magnet

S2.1a Indicate materials to be used and steps to follow to conduct the investigation and describe how data will be recorded (journal, dates and times, etc.)

Read Together and Learn

What do magnets do?

A magnet can **attract**, or pull, some objects. Magnets attract objects through solids, liquids, and gases. A very strong magnet can pull objects from far away. The farther a magnet is from the object, the weaker the magnet's pull will be.

Many magnets contain iron. Magnets attract objects containing iron. They can also attract objects made of nickel or steel.

The magnet pulls the paper clip without touching it.

Magnets are holding these objects in place.

buy:
— eggs
— milk

There are many objects that magnets cannot attract. These include plastic, wood, and some metals. Walk around your classroom with a magnet. See what the magnet attracts and what it does not.

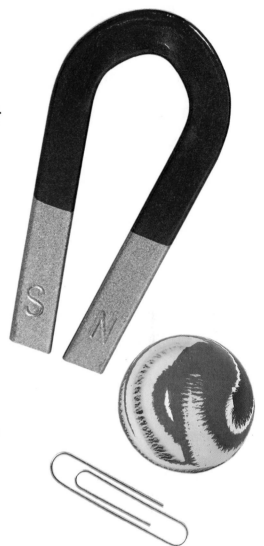

What a Magnet Attracts

object	attracts	does not attract
crayon		✓
screw	✓	
eraser		✓
lock	✓	

Read a Chart

Which objects will stick to a magnet?

✓ Will a magnet attract a button? Why or why not?

What are poles?

The two ends of a magnet are its **poles**. Every magnet has a north pole and a south pole. Put the north pole of one magnet next to the south pole of another. They will attract each other.

Now put the two south poles together. They will **repel** each other, or push apart. The same thing will happen with the two north poles. The push and pull of a magnet is strongest at its poles.

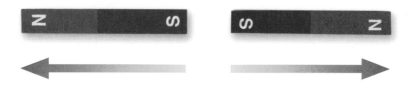

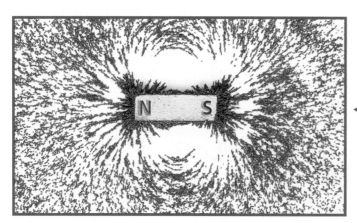

◄ **This magnet attracts tiny pieces of iron.**

≡Quick Lab

Cover the labels on two bar magnets. **Investigate** to find which poles are alike and which are different.

FACT ▷ Some magnets are much stronger than others.

Our planet Earth acts like a big magnet. Like every magnet, it has north and south poles.

A compass is a magnet that is free to spin. The north pole in the magnet points toward Earth's North Pole.

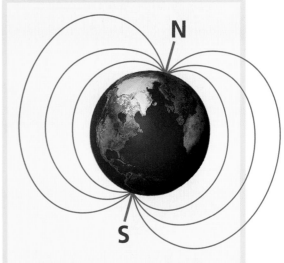

Earth has a magnetic force around the North Pole and South Pole.

The needle inside a compass is a magnet that points to Earth's North Pole.

 Where is the pull of a magnet strongest?

Think, Talk, and Write

1. **Problem and Solution.** Two magnets repel each other. How can you make them stick together?

2. What will a magnet attract?

3. Write about how you can tell if an object might be made of steel or iron.

Art Link

Make a poster that shows how people use magnets.

 e-Review Summaries and quizzes online at www.macmillanmh.com

Be a Scientist

paper clips

magnets

How can you compare the strength of different magnets?

Find out how many paper clips each of the magnets can attract.

What to Do

① Hang a paper clip from a magnet. Keep adding more clips in a line until no more will stick.

Step **①**

M2.Ia. Explain verbally, graphically, or in writing the reasoning used to develop mathematical conclusions

2 **Record Data.** Write how many paper clips can hang from the magnet.

3 Repeat the steps using different magnets.

4 **Communicate.** Make a bar graph to show the strengths of your magnets.

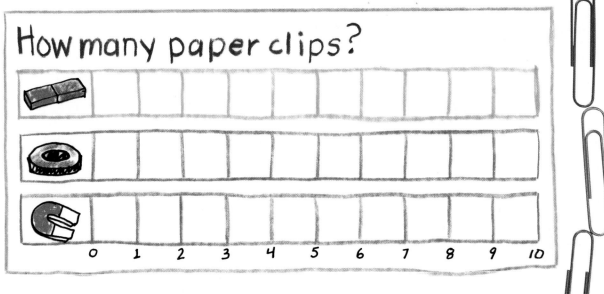

How many paper clips?

0 1 2 3 4 5 6 7 8 9 10

Investigate More

Investigate. How many paper clips can you pick up with two magnets? Find a way to attach two magnets and try it out.

Forces Every Day

Push! I use forces all day long. I push the heavy cart to make it move. A push is a force. I pull on the cart to make it stop. A pull is a force, too.

Plop! I crack an egg. A force called gravity makes the egg fall into the bowl. Objects move with different motions. I stir the pancake batter around and around.

Flip! I flip my pancakes. Simple machines can make work easier. A lever can change the direction of a force. The force makes the pancake fly through the air.

Yum! The pancake lands on my plate. Other things use pushes and pulls, too. A magnet keeps my shopping list on the refrigerator. It is time to buy more eggs and milk!

Vocabulary

Use each word once for items 1–6.

friction

gravity

lever

position

ramp

speed

1. When two objects rub together, they can be slowed down by _____.
PS-5.1 (d)

2. A simple machine that makes it easier to push an object to a higher level is a _____.
PS-5.1 (f)

3. We can tell where an object is by its _____.
PS-5.1 (a)

4. Objects fall to the floor because of a force called _____.
PS-5.1 (c); PS-5.2 (a)

5. How far an object moves in a period of time is called _____.
PS-5.

6. A simple machine that moves against a fulcrum is called a _____.
PS-5.1 (f)

Answer the questions below.

7. Summarize. Describe the position of the blue paper.
PS-5.I (a)

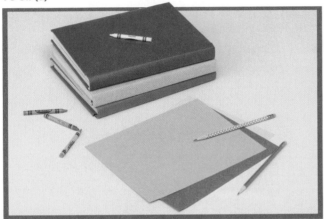

8. Investigate. What can help you move a heavy object?
PS-5.I (e)

9. What does gravity do?
PS-5.I (c); PS-5.2 (a)

I0. Describe some of the simple machines in this picture and how they work.
PS-5.I (f)

 The Big Idea

II. How do things move?
PS-4; PS-5

CHAPTER 8

Using Energy

The
**Big
Idea** How do we
use energy?

New Jersey amusent pier

Key Vocabulary

fuel something that gives off heat when it burns (page 301)

vibrate to move back and forth quickly (page 309)

current electricity a kind of energy that moves in a path (page 326)

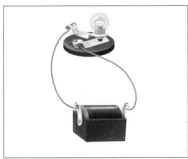

circuit a path that electricity flows in (page 326)

PS-3. Matter is made up of particles whose properties determine the observable characteristics of matter and its reactivity. **PS-4.** Energy exists in many forms, and when these forms change energy is conserved.

Heat

Look and Wonder

This is a desert on a sunny day.
How can you tell it is hot?

 PS-4.I (a,b,c,f). Describe a variety of forms of energy ... and the changes
that occur in objects when they interact with those forms of energy.
PS-4.2 (a). Observe the way one form of energy can be transferred into
another form of energy present in common situations....

Where will ice cubes melt more quickly?

What to Do

You need

ice cubes

① Fill two cups with equal amounts of ice. Place one cup in a sunny place. Place the other cup in a shady place.

2 cups

② **Predict.** Which cup of ice will melt first?

③ Record how long it takes for the ice in each cup to melt. Why did one cup of ice melt more quickly?

watch or clock

Explore More

④ **Predict.** Put equal amounts of water of the same temperature in two cups. How will each cup of water feel after one hour?

Step ①

sun   shade

S3.3a. Explain their findings to others, and actively listen to suggestions for possible interpretations and ideas

What is heat?

Energy makes matter move or change. There are many kinds of energy. **Heat** is a kind of energy that can change the state of matter. Heat can turn a solid to a liquid. Heat can turn a liquid to a gas.

We use heat every day. Most heat on Earth comes from the Sun. The Sun warms the air, land, and water on Earth.

On a hot day, the Sun warms the water and land first. Then the air becomes warm.

Heat comes from other things, too. **Fuel** is something that gives off heat when it burns. Gas, oil, wood, and coal can be burned as fuel.

Heat can also come from motion. Rub your hands together quickly to make them warm. Now touch your hands to your face. Heat moved from your hands to your face.

▲ **People use fuel to keep warm.**

▲ **People use fuel to cook food.**

✓ How is heat used in your school and home?

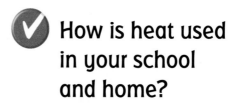

▲ **This motion makes heat.**

What is temperature?

Temperature is a measure of how hot or cold something is. We measure the temperature of air, water, even our bodies. To measure temperature, we use a tool called a thermometer. Some thermometers have a liquid inside. The liquid goes up or down with the temperature.

Temperature

Read a Photo

Is it hotter during the day or night? How can you tell?

Use a thermometer to **compare** the temperature of soil, water, and air.

soil water air

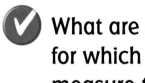 **What are some things for which you can measure temperature?**

Think, Talk, and Write

1. **Main Idea and Details.** Where does most of our heat come from?

2. How do we measure temperature?

3. Write about some ways people make heat.

Art Link

Look around your school or home for sources of heat. Draw them.

LOG ON e-**Review** Summaries and quizzes online at **www.macmillanmh.com**

Inquiry Skill: Measure

You measure to find out about things around you. You can measure how long, how heavy, or how warm something is.

▶ **Learn It**

A class wants to measure the temperature in different parts of their classroom. They measure the temperature by a sunny window. They measure the temperature in a shady place.

▲ **a sunny window**

They compare the temperatures after 15 minutes.

a sunny window	75°F
a shady place	70°F

▲ **a shady place**

▶ **Try It**

You can measure the temperature of ice, cold water, and warm water.

1. Fill cups with ice, cold water, and warm water.

2. Predict. What is the temperature in each cup? Record your predictions.

3. Measure. Put a thermometer in each cup for 5 minutes. Record each temperature.

4. Compare. Were your predictions close to your measurements?

Measuring Temperature			
	ice	cold	warm
predict			
measure			

M3.1a. Use appropriate scientific tools, such as metric rulers, spring scale, pan balance, graph paper, thermometers [Fahrenheit and Celsius], graduated cylinder to solve problems about the natural world

Sound

Look and Wonder

Keep the noise down! How are sounds made? How can some sounds be different from others?

PS-4.1 (a,d). Describe a variety of forms of energy ... and the changes that occur in objects when they interact with those forms of energy.
PS-4.2 (b). Observe the way one form of energy can be transferred into another form of energy present in common situations....

How is sound made?

What to Do

1. Tie the string to the paper clip. Make a hole in the bottom of the cup.

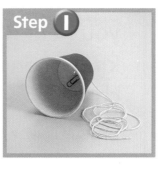
Step 1

string

2. Pull the string through the hole. The clip keeps the string from pulling through the cup.

paper cup

3. Wear goggles. Hold the cup and string with a partner. The third partner snaps the string.

goggles

4. **Observe.** What happens? How did you make sound?

Explore More

5. **Predict.** How will the sound be different if you change the length of the string? Try it.

paper clip

Step 3

Read Together and Learn

Vocabulary

sound

vibrate

pitch

SCIENCE QUEST   Explore sound with the Treasure Hunters.

What makes sound?

Ring! A loud alarm clock wakes you up each morning. How do you hear it? **Sound** is a kind of energy that we can hear.

▲ When the bells on the alarm clock are hit, they move back and forth quickly.

How We Hear Sound

▶ The guitar strings vibrate and make the air around them vibrate.

Sound energy is made when objects **vibrate**. When an object vibrates, it moves back and forth quickly. When something vibrates, air around the object vibrates also.

The eardrum is the part of our body we use to hear sounds. Messages sent from your ear to your brain tell you what sound you heard.

 How do you hear sounds?

▼ **These vibrations move to your eardrum so you can hear the sound of the guitar.**

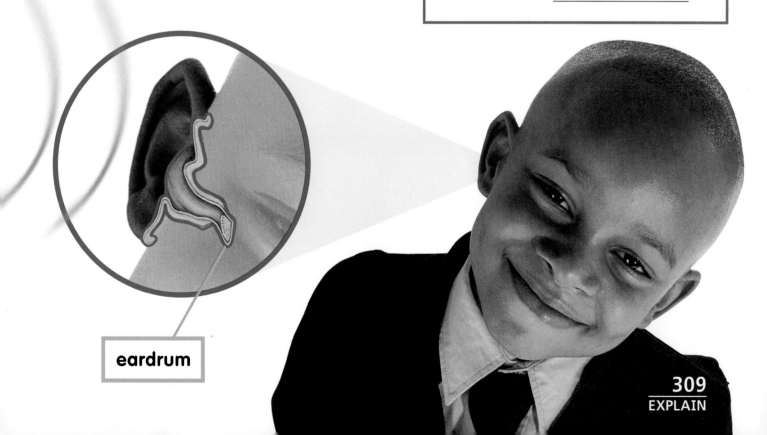

eardrum

How are sounds different?

Not all sounds are the same. You hear loud and soft sounds every day. You can make your voice loud or soft. A whisper has less energy than a shout. Try making loud and soft sounds.

▲ Small vibrations make soft sounds. The meow of a cat sounds soft.

▼ Big vibrations make loud sounds. The roar of a lion sounds loud.

Pitch is how high or low a sound is. Fast vibrations make sounds with a high pitch. Slow vibrations make sounds with a low pitch.

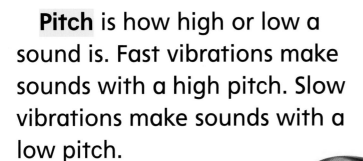

▶ **If you snap a short, tight string, it makes a high pitch.**

▶ **If you snap a long, loose string, it makes a low pitch.**

 How is a high pitch made?

harp

FACT Some sounds cannot be heard by humans.

What do sounds move through?

Place your ear against your desk. Now gently tap the desk with your pencil. You hear vibrations through the wood of the desk. Sound moves through solids, such as wood or plastic.

Sound moves through liquids also. Have you ever heard sound under water? The water vibrates and you hear sound.

▼ **Dolphins and other animals make sounds under water to communicate with each other.**

Most sounds you hear move through air. Air is made of gases. The closer you are to a sound, the louder it sounds. The farther you are from a sound, the softer it sounds.

▲ How can you tell when a fire engine is close by or far away?

 What can sounds move through?

Think, Talk, and Write

1. **Problem and Solution.** How would you get a guitar string to make a sound with a high pitch?

2. Why do your hands make a sound when you clap them together?

3. Write about how you would make a sound louder.

Music Link

Make your own musical instruments. Stretch rubber bands around a plastic cup. Vibrate the rubber bands to make different pitches.

LOG ON e-Review Summaries and quizzes online at www.macmillanmh.com

Sound Off!

Think about the sounds you hear every day. Some sounds are loud and others are soft. Some sounds are high and others are low.

 **Write About It**

Describe the pitch and volume of a sound you hear every day. How do we use sounds? Why are sounds important?

Remember

When you describe something, you give details.

LOG ON **e-Journal** Write about it online at **www.macmillanmh.com**

 S3.3a. Explain their findings to others, and actively listen to suggestions for possible interpretations and ideas

Drum Fun

Miss Lee sells four different drums in her store. The first drum is 10 centimeters wide. The second drum is 20 centimeters wide. The third drum is 30 centimeters wide.

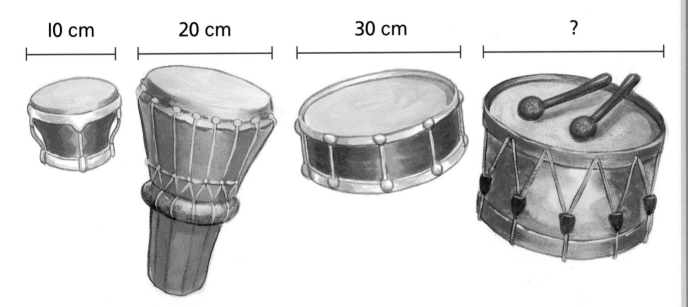

10 cm   20 cm   30 cm   ?

Follow the Pattern

How wide is the fourth drum?
Follow this number pattern:

10 + 10 = 20

20 + 10 = 30

30 + ? = ?

Miss Lee knows that the smallest drum has the highest pitch. Which drum has the lowest pitch?

Remember
You can use a pattern to help you solve problems.

M2.lb. Explain verbally, graphically, or in writing patterns and relationships observed in the physical and living environment

Light

Look and Wonder

Where is this light coming from?
What is blocking some of the light?

PS-3.1 (g). Observe and describe properties of materials, using appropriate tools. **PS-4.1 (d).** Describe a variety of forms of energy (e.g., heat, chemical, light) and the changes that occur in objects when they interact with those forms of energy.

What does light pass through?

What to Do

1. **Predict.** Which materials will light pass through? Which will block the light?

2. Work with a partner. Hold up the cardboard. Hold plastic wrap three inches in front of the board. Your partner shines the flashlight on the object.

3. **Observe.** Did the plastic wrap block the light or did the light pass through it?

4. **Compare.** Which objects block the light and which let light pass through?

Explore More

5. **Predict.** What might happen with other classroom items? Try it.

You need

flashlight

cardboard

plastic wrap

various items

Step 2

 S3.4a. State, orally and in writing, any inferences or generalizations indicated by the data, with appropriate modifications of their original prediction/explanation

317
EXPLORE

Vocabulary
light
reflect

What is light?

You need light to see things. **Light** is a kind of energy. You see things because light will **reflect**, or bounce off things around you. Light that reflects off objects enters your eyes. Then you can see the objects.

Some sources of light are the Sun, lightbulbs, and flashlights. Most light on Earth comes from the Sun.

Smooth, shiny objects such as mirrors reflect a lot of light.

Have you ever made a shadow on a wall? A shadow is a dark area where light does not reach.

Different objects let different amounts of light through. A book is a solid object. It can block light and make a shadow. Glass is clear. It does not make a shadow because light passes through it.

Shadows

Read a Photo

How is this shadow made?

 What are some sources of light?

How do we see color?

Did you know light can bend? Light is a mix of all colors. When white light bends, it separates into different colors. Then we can see the colors of the rainbow.

A prism is an object that can make light bend.

Quick Lab

Use a prism and sunlight to see the colors of the rainbow. **Observe** and draw what you see.

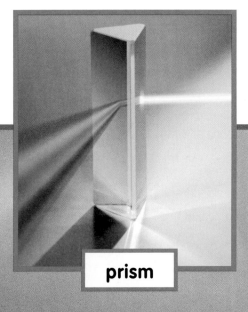

prism

Raindrops can act like prisms and separate light to make rainbows.

Have you ever seen colored lights? A filter is a tool that lets only certain colors of light pass through it.

Some filters let only one color pass through. A red filter blocks all colors except red. You see only red light with a red filter.

Colored glass makes a white light look red, green, or yellow.

✓ What color is most light we see?

Think, Talk, and Write

1. **Sequence.** What happens when we see objects?

2. What kind of objects make shadows?

 3. Write a list of things that light cannot pass through.

Art Link

Make a filter. Cover a flashlight with colored plastic wrap. Then make shadow puppets!

LOG ON ⓔ-Review Summaries and quizzes online at **www.macmillanmh.com**

You need

black cloth

white cloth

2 thermometers

clock

How does sunlight affect the temperature of light and dark objects?

What to Do

1. Record the temperature of each thermometer on a chart. Wrap one thermometer in black cloth as shown. Wrap the other in white cloth.

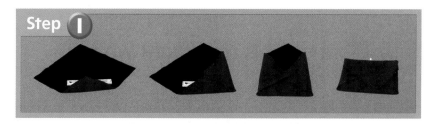

Step 1

2. Place the wrapped thermometers on a sunny windowsill. Wait 15 minutes.

Step 2

③ **Compare.** Feel each cloth with your hands after 15 minutes. Which color cloth feels warmer?

Step ③

④ **Predict.** Which color will have the higher temperature? Why do you think so?

⑤ **Record Data.** Unwrap each cloth and record each temperature on the chart.

⑥ **Compare** the temperatures. What happened to the temperature of each cloth? Was your prediction correct?

Investigate More

Compare. What other dark colors and light colors can you test? Make a plan and test it.

M3.la. Use appropriate scientific tools, such as metric rulers, spring scale, pan balance, graph paper, thermometers [Fahrenheit and Celsius], graduated cylinder to solve problems about the natural world

Exploring Electricity

the Bay Bridge in San Francisco, California

Look and Wonder

How do you think these lights get their energy?

PS-4.1 (d,e,g). Describe a variety of forms of energy ... and the changes that occur in objects when they interact with those forms of energy.
PS-4.2 (b). Observe the way one form of energy can be transferred into another form of energy present in common situations....

What makes the bulb light up?

What to Do

① **Predict.** Look at the battery, bulb, and wires. How could you put them together to light the bulb? Record your ideas with a partner.

② △ **Be Careful.** Try your ideas. Which of your ideas made the bulb light? Which ideas did not work?

③ **Record Data.** Write down your results with your partner. How many ways did you make the bulb light up?

Explore More

④ **Predict.** How could you make a second bulb light up? What else would you need?

You need

wire

battery

lightbulb

Step ②

What is current electricity?

Do batteries make some of your toys work? Batteries make a kind of electricity. **Current electricity** is a kind of energy that moves in a path. The electricity moves along a path called a **circuit**. The circuit needs to be completely connected for the electricity to move. Electricity moves better through some materials than others. This property is called *conductivity.*

Circuit

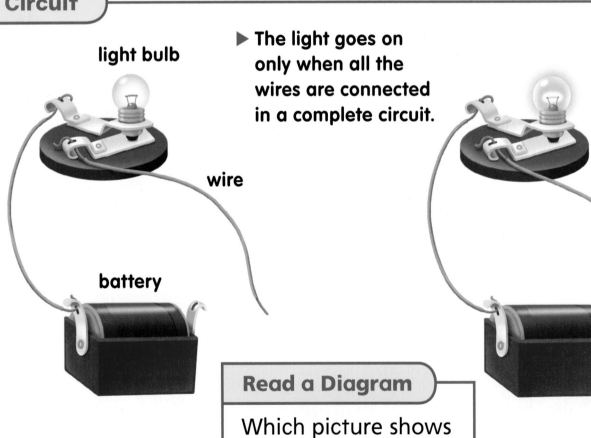

light bulb

wire

battery

▶ **The light goes on only when all the wires are connected in a complete circuit.**

Read a Diagram

Which picture shows a complete circuit?

Current electricity can be changed into heat, light, or sound energy. It can also make things move. Current electricity can come from batteries or from outlets in the wall.

Buildings called power plants change other kinds of energy into electricity. The electricity runs through wires into your house and into the outlets. When you plug in your toaster and turn it on, you complete the circuit with the power plant.

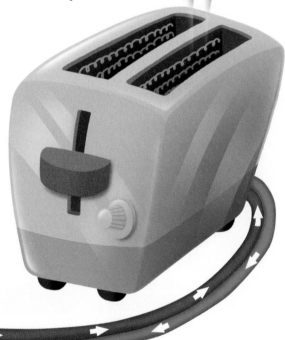

▶ **Electricity can move through the circuit when the toaster is plugged in.**

 How do you use current electricity every day?

FACT ▶ Electricity comes from power plants through wires, not from your wall.

What is static electricity?

You take your clothes out of the dryer. They are stuck together! This happens because of static electricity.

Static electricity is a kind of energy made by tiny pieces of matter. You cannot see these pieces of matter, but they are everywhere.

When tiny pieces of matter attract or repel each other, they have a charge.

Lightning is static electricity. Charges made in a storm jump between the clouds and the ground.

Like a magnet some of these pieces of matter stick together. Others push apart.

Charges can build up on one object and jump to another. Sometimes you can see or hear a static charge move from one object to another.

 What are some examples of static electricity?

The cat's fur is attracted to the charged balloon, so it sticks up.

Think, Talk, and Write

1. **Cause and Effect.** How does a battery make your toy work?

2. What kind of energy causes your socks to stick together?

3. Write about what your day would be like without electricity.

Social Studies Link

Research and write about how people use electricity.

It's Electric

You can flip a switch to turn on a light, a computer, or a dishwasher. They all use electricity.

The electricity starts at a power plant. At the plant, energy turns a large wheel called a turbine. The energy might come from burning coal or oil, flowing water, wind, or nuclear reactions.

POWER PLANT

coal burning coal turbine generator

S3.Ia. Accurately transfer data from a science journal or notes to appropriate graphic organizer

The turbine turns a magnet inside a machine called a generator. The generator makes electricity.

When you flip a switch in your home, you make a circuit with the power plant. Then electricity flows through power lines and stations to the plug in your home and into your lamp.

Electricity leaves the power plant and travels through many power lines.

Electricity comes to my home.

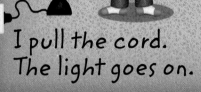

I pull the cord. The light goes on.

Talk About It

Cause and Effect. What makes the light go on in your home?

AMERICAN MUSEUM OF NATURAL HISTORY

Energy Poem

Some energy can be seen.
Some energy can be felt.
Heat is a kind of energy that
can make solids melt.

Sound is a kind of energy.
I hear pitches high and low.
I hear because of vibrations,
small, big, fast, and slow.

Light is a kind of energy.
Light can bounce and bend.
I block light to make shadows.
I see white when all colors blend.

Electricity is a kind of energy.
It makes many things run.
Without electricity, my toy
would be no fun!

Vocabulary

Use each word once for items 1–5.

circuit
current electricity
reflect
static electricity
vibrate

1. Sound is made when objects
_____.

PS-4.1 (a,d)

2. Energy that moves through wires
is called _____.

PS-4.1 (a,b,e)

3. Energy that jumps from cloud to
cloud is called _____.

PS-4.1 (b)

4. When light bounces off objects,
the light will _____.

PS-4.1 (d)

5. This picture shows a complete
_____.

PS-4.1 (b,d,e); PS-4.2 (b)

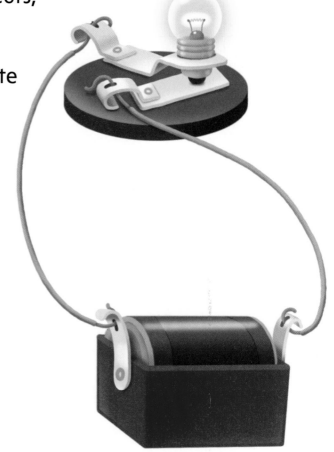

Answer the questions below.

6. What happens to a sound when it moves away from you?

7. **Measure.** How many degrees Celsius is the temperature?
PS-3.I (c,d,e); PS-4.I (a)

8. What can heat do?
PS-4.I (a,c,d,f,g)

9. **Main Idea and Details.** Why can you see a rainbow with a prism?
PS-4.I (a,d)

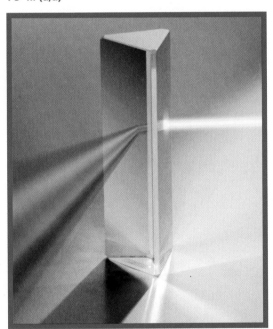

10. How do we use energy?
PS-3; PS-4

Popcorn Hop

by Stephanie Calmenson

Everybody do the popcorn dance!

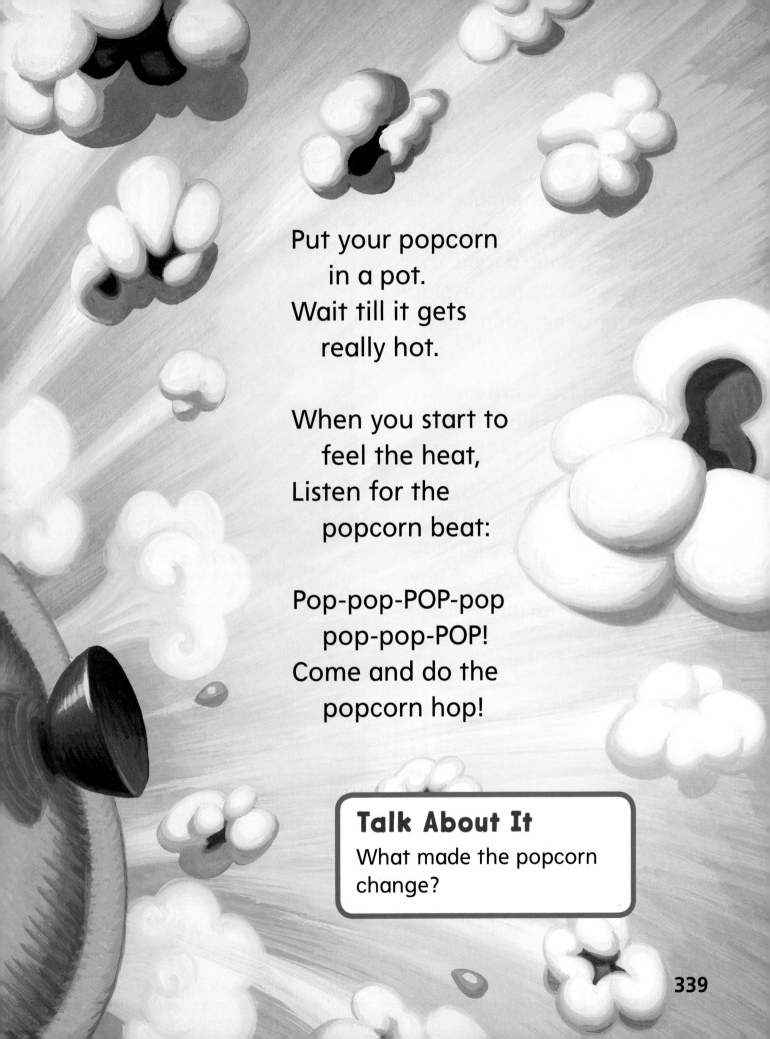

Put your popcorn
in a pot.
Wait till it gets
really hot.

When you start to
feel the heat,
Listen for the
popcorn beat:

Pop-pop-POP-pop
pop-pop-POP!
Come and do the
popcorn hop!

Talk About It
What made the popcorn
change?

339

Careers in Science

Food Chemist

Would you like to make your own cereal or flavor of juice? You could become a food chemist. Food chemists explore ways to make new and more delicious foods.

Food chemists learn how to make yogurt smooth. They find out how to keep cereal crunchy. They might find a way to freeze vegetables so they taste fresher. Food chemists have to understand the science of how food products are made.

food chemist

More Careers to Think About

nutritionist

chef

Reference

Science Handbook

Health Handbook

Glossary

New York State Standards

Measurements

Nonstandard

You can use objects to measure the length of some solids. Line up objects and count them. Use objects that are alike. They must be the same size.

▲ This string is about 8 paper clips long.

▲ This string is about 2 hands long.

Try It

Measure a solid in your classroom.
Tell how you did it.

Standard

You can also use a ruler to measure the length of some solids. You can measure in a unit called **centimeters**.

◀ **This toy is about 8 centimeters long. This is written as 8 cm.**

centimeters

You can also use a ruler to measure in a unit called **inches**. One inch is longer than I centimeter.

◀ **This toy is about 3 inches long. This is written as 3 in.**

inches

Try It

Estimate the length of this toy car. Then find its exact length.

Measurements

Volume

You can measure the volume of a liquid with a **measuring cup**. Volume is the amount of space a liquid takes up.

▲ This measuring cup has 1 cup of liquid.

Mass

You can measure mass with a **balance**. The side that has the object with more mass will go down.

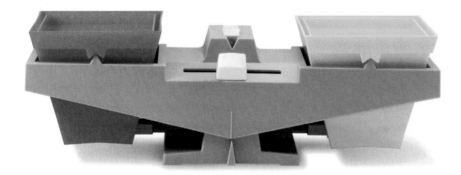

▲ Before you compare the mass of two objects, be sure the arrow points to the line.

Try It

Place two objects on a balance. Which has more mass?

Time

You can measure time with a **clock**. A clock measures in units called hours, minutes, and seconds. There are 60 minutes in I hour.

minute hand

hour hand

There are 5 minutes between each number.

Temperature

Degrees Fahrenheit

Degrees Celsius

You can measure temperature with a **thermometer**. Thermometers measure in units called degrees.

◄ The temperature is 85 degrees Fahrenheit.

Try It

Use a thermometer to find the temperature outside today.

Science Tools

Computer

A computer is a tool that can help you get information. You can use the Internet to connect to other computers around the world.

When you use a computer, make sure an adult knows what you are working on.

monitor

hard drive

keyboard

mouse

Hand Lens

A hand lens is another tool that can help you get information. A hand lens makes objects seem larger.

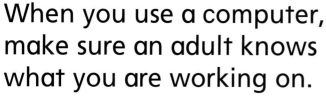

Try It

Use a hand lens to look at an object. Draw what you see.

Graphs

Bar Graphs

Bar graphs organize data. The title of the graph tells you what the data is about. The shaded bars tell you how much of each thing there is.

Favorite Fruits

0 1 2 3 4 5

Try It

Make a bar graph that shows your classmates' favorite fruits.

Your Body

Skeletal System

Your body has many parts. All your parts work together to help you live.

Bones are hard body parts inside your body. They help you stand straight. Your bones give your body its shape.

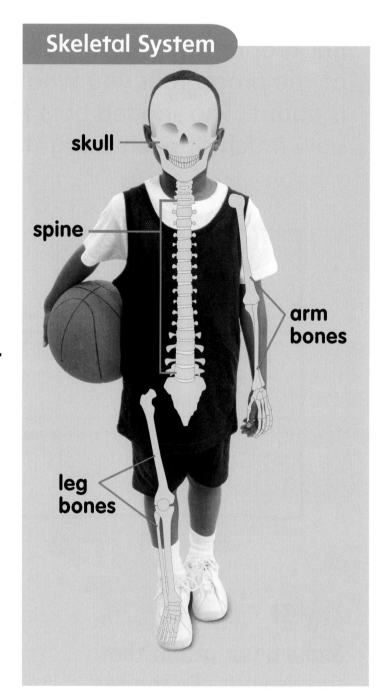

Skeletal System

skull

spine

arm bones

leg bones

Try It

How many bones do you think there are in your arms? Count them.

Muscular System

Muscles are body parts that help you move. They are inside your body.

Muscles get stronger when you exercise them.

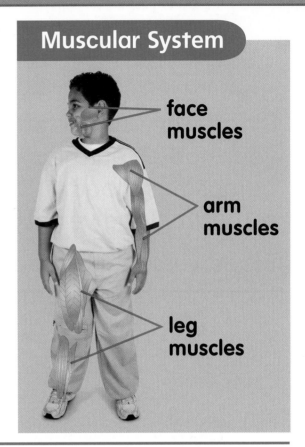

Muscular System

face muscles

arm muscles

leg muscles

Nervous System

Your brain sends messages all around your body. The messages travel along tiny body parts called nerves.

These messages tell your body parts to move. They can also alert you of danger.

Try It

Jump up and down in place. Which muscles did you use?

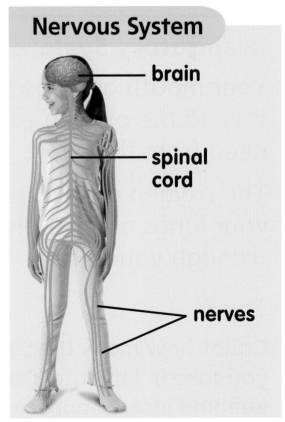

Nervous System

brain

spinal cord

nerves

Your Body

Circulatory System

Blood travels through your body. Your heart pumps this blood through blood vessels.

Blood vessels are tubes that carry blood inside your body. Arteries and veins are blood vessels.

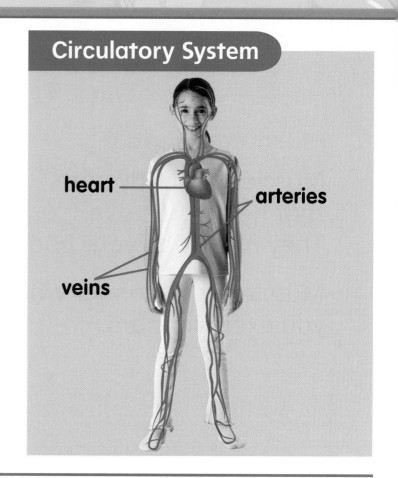

Circulatory System

heart

arteries

veins

Respiratory System

Your mouth and nose take in the oxygen you need from the air.

The oxygen goes into your lungs and travels through your blood.

Try It

Count how many breaths you take in 1 minute. Do ten jumping jacks. Count again.

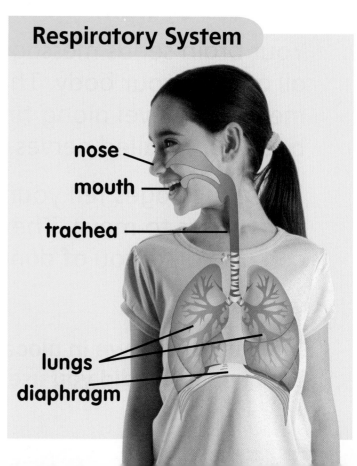

Respiratory System

nose

mouth

trachea

lungs

diaphragm

Digestive System

When you eat, your body uses food for energy. Food enters your body through your mouth. Your stomach and intestines help you get nutrients from the food in your body.

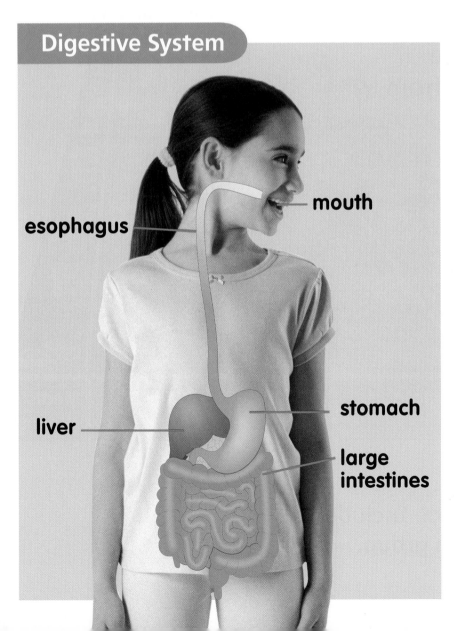

Digestive System

esophagus

mouth

liver

stomach

large intestines

Try It

Write a story about why your body needs food.

Healthful Foods

MyPyramid

MyPyramid is a guide for healthful eating. A healthful meal contains foods from the five food groups. A food group is a group of foods that are alike.

Eat more foods from the largest slice of the pyramid. Eat less from the smallest slice.

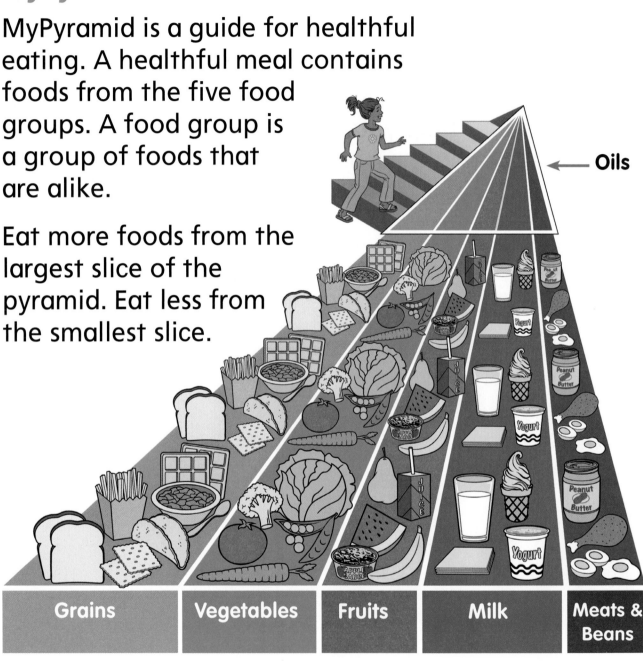

Oils

| Grains | Vegetables | Fruits | Milk | Meats & Beans |

Try It

Plan a healthful meal. Include one food from each group.

Healthful Foods

Nutrients are materials in foods that make you healthy. Nutrients called carbohydrates store energy in your body. Proteins help your body grow.

chickpeas

People around the world get nutrients from different foods.

Foods Around the World

Food	Parts of the world	Nutrient
Rice	Asia	carbohydrate
Tortilla	Central America	carbohydrate
Millet	Africa	carbohydrate
chickpeas	Middle East	protein
olives	Europe	oils

rice

olives

Try It

List your favorite foods. Find out what nutrients are in the food.

Stay Healthy

Be active every day. Exercise keeps your heart and lungs healthy.

Doctors and dentists can help you stay healthy as you grow.

▲ Exercise is important for a healthy body.

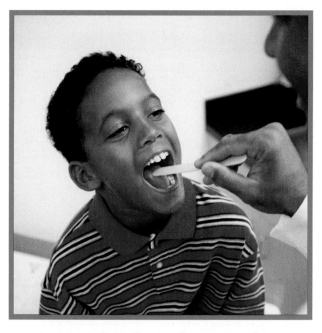

▲ Get a checkup from a doctor and dentist every year.

Try It

Record how many times you exercise in one week.

Take Care of Your Body

Tobacco and alcohol harm you.
Tobacco smoke can make it hard
to breathe. Alcohol slows down
your mind and body.

**Here are some ways to
take care of your body. ▼**

▲ **Only take medicines
that your parent
or doctor gives you.**

Take Care of Yourself

Take a bath.

Brush and floss
your teeth every day.

Stand up straight.

Get plenty of sleep.

Try It

Make a poster about
being drug free. Share
it with your school.

Safety Indoors

To stay safe indoors, do not touch dangerous things. Tell an adult about them right away. Never taste anything without permission.

In case of a fire, get out fast. If your clothes catch fire, remember to stop, drop, and roll.

Try It

Practice stop, drop, and roll. Teach it to a friend.

▲ **Do not touch these things.**

stop

drop

roll

Safety Outdoors

Be safe outdoors. Follow these rules.

▲ Wear a helmet.

▲ Cross at a crosswalk.

▲ Wear your seat belt.

▲ Follow game rules.

Try It

Choose one of the rules. Make
a poster showing the safety rule.

Wind Scale

Very windy weather can be dangerous. Do not play outdoors before a storm. Scientists use a scale like this one to tell how hard the wind is blowing.

▼ **This is a Beaufort scale.**

Wind Scale		
Number	**What You Can See**	**Wind Speeds**
0	calm	less than 1 mile per hour
3	gentle breeze	8–12 miles per hour
6	strong breeze	25–30 miles per hour
9	very strong wind	47–54 miles per hour
12	hurricane	more than 73 miles per hour

Try It

Look out a window. What kind of wind do you see? Use the wind scale to help.

Glossary

A

adaptation Body part or a way an animal acts that helps it stay alive. (page 78) **The anteater's long snout is an adaptation.**

amphibian Animal that lives part of its life in water and part on land. (page 63) **A salamander is an amphibian.**

anemometer A tool that measures the speed of wind. (page 139) **The stronger the wind is, the faster the anemometer spins.**

attract To pull toward something. (page 284) **A magnet can attract some objects.**

axis A center line that an object spins around. (page 169) **Earth spins on its axis.**

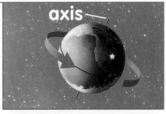

C

camouflage A way that animals blend into their surroundings. (page 79) **Animals use camouflage to stay safe.**

chemical change   When matter changes into different matter. (page 236) **Cooking an egg makes a chemical change.**

circuit   A path that electricity flows in. (page 326) **A bulb will light when connected with wires in a circuit.**

cirrus   Thin, wispy clouds high in the sky. (page 153) **The wind blows cirrus clouds into wispy streams.**

condense   To change from a gas to a liquid. (pages 145, 243) **Water vapor can condense on a cold glass.**

cumulus   White, puffy clouds. (page 152) **Small cumulus clouds appear in good weather.**

current electricity   A kind of energy that moves in a path. (page 326) **When you use a toaster, you use current electricity.**

D

drought A long period of time with little or no rain. (page 110) **Plants can die in a drought.**

E

endangered When many of one kind of animal die and only a few are left. (page 112) **These tigers are endangered.**

evaporate To change from a liquid to a gas. (pages 144, 243) **Water can evaporate from oceans, rivers, lakes, or land.**

extinct When a living thing dies out and no more of its kind live on Earth. (page 115) **Dinosaurs are extinct.**

F

flower Plant part that makes seeds. (page 34) **Some flowers can grow into fruit.**

food chain A model of the order in which living things get the food they need. (page 102) **A food chain begins with the Sun.**

food web Two or more food chains that are connected. (page 105) **This picture shows a desert food web.**

force A push or pull on an object. (page 267) **When you kick a ball, you are using a kind of force.**

fossil What is left of a living thing from the past. (page 114) **This fish fossil was found in the desert.**

friction A force that slows down moving things. (page 270) **A skate makes friction when the wheels rub against the ground.**

fuel Material burned to make power or heat. (page 301) **Wood is fuel for fire.**

fulcrum The point that a lever moves against. (page 276) **This piece of wood can act as a fulcrum.**

fulcrum

G

gas Matter that spreads to fill the space it is in. (page 228) **The tube is filled with gas.**

gravity A kind of force that pulls down on everything on Earth. (page 269) **Gravity is the force that pulls a ball to the ground.**

H

habitat A place where plants and animals live. (page 94) **A habitat can be wet, dry, windy, or cold.**

heat Kind of energy that makes objects warmer. (page 300) **The Sun gives us heat.**

I

insect Animal with six legs, antennae, and a hard outer shell. (page 64) **An ant is an insect.**

L

larva Stage in the life cycle of some animals after they hatch from an egg. (page 72) **A caterpillar is a larva.**

lever   A simple machine made of a bar that turns around a point. (page 276) **A lever can help you move or lift objects.**

life cycle   How a living thing grows, lives, has young, and dies. (pages 40, 70) **The pictures show the life cycle of a chicken.**

light   A kind of energy that lets us see. (page 318) **We get light from the Sun.**

liquid   Matter that takes the shape of the container it is in. (page 226) **Water is a liquid.**

mammal   Animal with hair or fur that feeds milk to its young. (page 62) **A lion is a mammal.**

mass   The amount of matter in an object. (page 210) **The larger boot has more mass.**

matter Anything that takes up space and has mass. (page 210) **Everything around us is made of matter.**

minerals Bits of rock and soil that help plants and animals grow. (pages 26) **Plants use minerals in the ground to grow.**

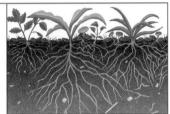

motion A change in the position of an object. (page 259) **This dog is in motion.**

O

orbit The path Earth takes around the Sun. (page 178) **Earth orbits the Sun each year.**

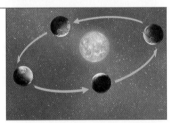

oxygen A gas found in the air we breathe. (page 31) **Living things need oxygen.**

P

phase The Moon's shape as we see it from Earth. (page 187) **The Moon's phase will change each night.**

physical change   A change in the size or shape of matter. (page 234) **When you fold matter, you make a physical change.**

pitch   How high or low a sound is. (page 311) **Short, tight strings make a high pitch.**

high pitch
low pitch

poles   The two ends of a magnet, or either end of Earth's axis. (page 286) **Earth has two poles, a north pole and a south pole.**

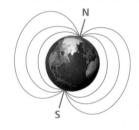

N
S

pollen   Sticky powder inside a flower that helps make seeds. (page 36) **Pollen can move from flower to flower.**

pollen

position   The place where something is. (page 258) **The position of the dog is above the cat.**

precipitation   Water falling from the sky as rain, snow, or hail. (page 137) **Rain is one kind of precipitation.**

predator An animal that hunts other animals for food. (page 103) **A predator must be fast to catch its food.**

prey Animals that are eaten by predators. (page 103) **The bird catches prey in its beak.**

property The look, feel, smell, sound, or taste of a thing. (page 212) **One property of this toy toucan is that it is soft.**

pupa Stage in a butterfly life cycle when a caterpillar makes a hard case around itself. (page 72) **The pupa hangs from a branch.**

R

ramp A simple machine with a flat, slanted surface. (page 277) **A ramp can be used to move an object from one level to another.**

reflect To bounce off something. (page 318) **Light can reflect better off shiny objects.**

repel To push away or apart. (page 286)
The two south poles of a magnet repel each other.

reptile Animal with rough, scaly skin. (page 63) **An alligator is a reptile.**

rotation A turn or spin. (page 168) **Earth makes one rotation in 24 hours.**

S

seed Plant part that can grow into a new plant. (page 30) **A seed can grow with water, warmth, and air.**

seedling A young plant. (page 34) **A seedling will grow into an adult plant.**

simple machine A tool that can change the size or direction of a force. (page 276) **This simple machine is called a ramp.**

solid Matter that has a shape of its own. (page 218) **This chair is a solid.**

sound A type of energy that is heard when objects vibrate. (page 308) **An alarm clock makes a loud sound.**

speed How far something moves in a certain amount of time. (page 260) A **cheetah has a fast running speed.**

star An object in space made of hot, glowing gases. (page 188) **The Sun is a star that we see during the day.**

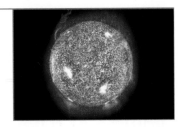

static electricity A kind of energy made by tiny pieces of matter that attract and repel each other. (page 328) **Static electricity makes the cat's hair stick to the balloon.**

stratus Thin clouds that form into layers like sheets. (page 153) **Stratus clouds can cover the whole sky.**

LOG ON e-Glossary at www.macmillanmh.com

T

temperature   A measurement of how hot or cold something is. (page 136) **A low temperature means something is cold.**

trait   The way a living thing looks or acts. (page 47) **The color of a flower is a trait.**

V

vibrate   To move back and forth quickly. (page 309) **Strings vibrate to make sound.**

volume   The amount of space something takes up. (page 227) **You can measure the volume of a liquid with measuring cups.**

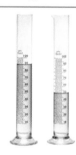

Science Skills

classify To group things by how they are alike. (page 5) **You can classify animals by how many legs they have.**

---

communicate To write, draw, or tell your ideas. (page 9) **You can communicate the ways you can change a piece of clay.**

Changing Clay
1. I roll the clay.
2. I pinched the clay.
3. I squeezed the clay.
4. I poked the clay.

---

compare To observe how things are alike or different. (page 5) **You can compare how a cat and a dog are alike and different.**

cats   alike   dogs
meow   4   bark
rough   legs   wet
tongue whiskers nose

---

draw conclusions To use what you observe to explain what happens. (page 9) **You can draw conclusions about why the stick will make a shadow.**

---

infer To use what you know to figure something out. (page 7) **From these tracks, you can infer which animal was here.**

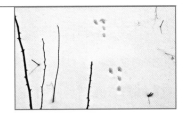

---

investigate To make a plan and try it out. (page 8) **You can investigate how long it takes the car to stop rolling.**

make a model To make something to show how something looks. (page 4) **You can make a model of a mountain in the ocean.**

measure To find out how far something moves, or how long, how much, or how warm something is. (page 6) **You can measure temperature with a thermometer.**

observe To see, hear, taste, touch, or smell. (page 4) **You can observe how the flower looks, smells, and feels.**

predict To use what you know to tell what you think will happen. (page 8) **You can predict what the weather will be like today.**

put things in order To tell or show what happens first, next, or last. (page 7) **You can put things in order to show the life cycle of a plant.**

record data To write down what you observe. (page 6) **You can record data about what your class had for lunch.**

Science Content Standards

STANDARD 1 – Analysis, Inquiry, and Design

MATHEMATICAL ANALYSIS

Key Idea 1: Abstraction and symbolic representation are used to communicate mathematically.

M1.1 Use special mathematical notation and symbolism to communicate in mathematics and to compare and describe quantities, express relationships, and relate mathematics to their immediate environment.

M1.1a Use plus, minus, greater than, less than, equal to, multiplication, and division signs

M1.1b Select the appropriate operation to solve mathematical problems

M1.1c Apply mathematical skills to describe the natural world

Key Idea 2: Deductive and inductive reasoning are used to reach mathematical conclusions.

M2.1 Use simple logical reasoning to develop conclusions, recognizing that patterns and relationships present in the environment assist them in reaching these conclusions.

M2.1a Explain verbally, graphically, or in writing the reasoning used to develop mathematical conclusions

M2.1b Explain verbally, graphically, or in writing patterns and relationships observed in the physical and living environment

Key Idea 3: Critical thinking skills are used in the solution of mathematical problems.

M3.1 Explore and solve problems generated from school, home, and community situations, using concrete objects or manipulative materials when possible.

M3.1a Use appropriate scientific tools, such as metric rulers, spring scale, pan balance, graph paper, thermometers [Fahrenheit and Celsius], graduated cylinder to solve problems about the natural world

SCIENTIFIC INQUIRY

Key Idea 1: The central purpose of scientific inquiry is to develop explanations of natural phenomena in a continuing, creative process.

S1.1 Ask "why" questions in attempts to seek greater understanding concerning objects and events they have observed and heard about.

S1.1a Observe and discuss objects and events and record observations

S1.1b Articulate appropriate questions based on observations

S1.2 Question the explanations they hear from others and read about, seeking clarification and comparing them with their own observations and understandings.

S1.2a Identify similarities and differences between explanations received from others or in print and personal observations or understandings

S1.3 Develop relationships among observations to construct descriptions of objects and events and to form their own tentative explanations of what they have observed.

S1.3a Clearly express a tentative explanation or description which can be tested

Key Idea 2: Beyond the use of reasoning and consensus, scientific inquiry involves the testing of proposed explanations involving the use of conventional techniques and procedures and usually requiring considerable ingenuity.

S2.1 Develop written plans for exploring phenomena or for evaluating explanations guided by questions or proposed explanations they have helped formulate.

S2.1a Indicate materials to be used and steps to follow to conduct the investigation and describe how data will be recorded (journal, dates and times, etc.)

S2.2 Share their research plans with others and revise them based on their suggestions.

S2.2a Explain the steps of a plan to others, actively listening to their suggestions for possible modification of the plan, seeking clarification and understanding of the suggestions and modifying the plan where appropriate

S2.3 Carry out their plans for exploring phenomena through direct observation and through the use of simple instruments that permit measurement of quantities, such as length, mass, volume, temperature, and time.

S2.3a Use appropriate "inquiry and process skills" to collect data

S2.3b Record observations accurately and concisely

Key Idea 3: The observations made while testing proposed explanations, when analyzed using conventional and invented methods, provide new insights into phenomena.

S3.1 Organize observations and measurements of objects and events through classification and the preparation of simple charts and tables.

S3.1a Accurately transfer data from a science journal or notes to appropriate graphic organizer

S3.2 Interpret organized observations and measurements, recognizing simple patterns, sequences, and relationships.

S3.2a State, orally and in writing, any inferences or generalizations indicated by the data collected

Science Content Standards

S3.3 Share their findings with others and actively seek their interpretations and ideas.

    S3.3a Explain their findings to others, and actively listen to suggestions for possible interpretations and ideas

S3.4 Adjust their explanations and understandings of objects and events based on their findings and new ideas.

    S3.4a State, orally and in writing, any inferences or generalizations indicated by the data, with appropriate modifications of their original prediction/explanation

    S3.4b State, orally and in writing, any new questions that arise from their investigation

ENGINEERING DESIGN

Key Idea 1: Engineering design is an iterative process involving modeling and optimization (finding the best solution within given constraints); this process is used to develop technological solutions to problems within given constraints.

T1.1 Describe objects, imaginary or real, that might be modeled or made differently and suggest ways in which the objects can be changed, fixed, or improved.

    T1.1a Identify a simple/common object which might be improved and state the purpose of the improvement

    T1.1b Identify features of an object that help or hinder the performance of the object

    T1.1c Suggest ways the object can be made differently, fixed, or improved within given constraints

T1.2 Investigate prior solutions and ideas from books, magazines, family, friends, neighbors, and community members.

    T1.2a Identify appropriate questions to ask about the design of an object

    T1.2b Identify the appropriate resources to use to find out about the design of an object

    T1.2c Describe prior designs of the object

T1.3 Generate ideas for possible solutions, individually and through group activity; apply age-appropriate mathematics and science skills; evaluate the ideas and determine the best solution; and explain reasons for the choices.

    T1.3a List possible solutions, applying age-appropriate math and science skills

    T1.3b Develop and apply criteria to evaluate possible solutions

    T1.3c Select a solution consistent with given constraints and explain why it was chosen

T1.4 Plan and build, under supervision, a model of the solution, using familiar materials, processes, and hand tools.

T1.4a Create a grade-appropriate graphic or plan listing all materials needed, showing sizes of parts, indicating how things will fit together, and detailing steps for assembly

T1.4b Build a model of the object, modifying the plan as necessary

T1.5 Discuss how best to test the solution; perform the test under teacher supervision; record and portray results through numerical and graphic means; discuss orally why things worked or didn't work; and summarize results in writing, suggesting ways to make the solution better.

    T1.5a Determine a way to test the finished solution or model

    T1.5b Perform the test and record the results, numerically and/or graphically

    T1.5c Analyze results and suggest how to improve the solution or model, using oral, graphic, or written formats

Students will understand and apply scientific concepts, principles, and theories pertaining to the physical setting and living environment and recognize the historical development of ideas in science.

STANDARD 4: The Physical Setting

Key Idea 1: The Earth and celestial phenomena can be described by principles of relative motion and perspective.

Performance Indicator 1.1: Describe patterns of daily, monthly, and seasonal changes in their environment.

Major Understandings:

1.1a Natural cycles and patterns include:
- Earth spinning around once every 24 hours (rotation), resulting in day and night
- Earth moving in a path around the Sun (revolution), resulting in one Earth year
- the length of daylight and darkness varying with the seasons
- weather changing from day to day and through the seasons
- the appearance of the Moon changing as it moves in a path around Earth to complete a single cycle

1.1b Humans organize time into units based on natural motions of Earth:
- second, minute, hour
- week, month

1.1c The Sun and other stars appear to move in a recognizable pattern both daily and seasonally.

Key Idea 2: Many of the phenomena that we observe on Earth involve interactions among components of air, water, and land.

Performance Indicator 2.1: Describe the relationship among air, water, and land on Earth.

Major Understandings:

2.1a Weather is the condition of the outside air at a particular moment.

2.1b Weather can be described and measured by:
- temperature
- wind speed and direction
- form and amount of precipitation
- general sky conditions (cloudy, sunny, partly cloudy)

2.1c Water is recycled by natural processes on Earth.
- evaporation: changing of water (liquid) into water vapor (gas)
- condensation: changing of water vapor (gas) into water (liquid)
- precipitation: rain, sleet, snow, hail
- runoff: water flowing on Earth's surface
- groundwater: water that moves downward into the ground

2.1d Erosion and deposition result from the interaction among air, water, and land.
- interaction between air and water breaks down earth materials
- pieces of earth material may be moved by air, water, wind, and gravity
- pieces of earth material will settle or deposit on land or in the water in different places
- soil is composed of broken-down pieces of living and nonliving earth material

2.1e Extreme natural events (floods, fires, earthquakes, volcanic eruptions, hurricanes, tornadoes, and other severe storms) may have positive or negative impacts on living things.

Key Idea 3: Matter is made up of particles whose properties determine the observable characteristics of matter and its reactivity.

Performance Indicator 3.1: Observe and describe properties of materials, using appropriate tools.

Major Understandings:

3.1a Matter takes up space and has mass. Two objects cannot occupy the same place at the same time.

3.1b Matter has properties (color, hardness, odor, sound, taste, etc.) that can be observed through the senses.

3.1c Objects have properties that can be observed, described, and/or measured: length, width, volume, size, shape, mass or weight, temperature, texture, flexibility, reflectiveness of light.

3.1d Measurements can be made with standard metric units and nonstandard units. (Note: Exceptions to the metric system usage are found in meteorology.)

3.1e The material(s) an object is made up of determine some specific properties of the object (sink/float, conductivity, magnetism). Properties can be observed or measured with tools such as hand lenses, metric rulers, thermometers, balances, magnets, circuit testers, and graduated cylinders.

3.1f Objects and/or materials can be sorted or classified according to their properties.

3.1g Some properties of an object are dependent on the conditions of the present surroundings in which the object exists. For example:
- temperature - hot or cold
- lighting - shadows, color
- moisture - wet or dry

Performance Indicator 3.2: Describe chemical and physical changes, including changes in states of matter.

Major Understandings:

3.2a Matter exists in three states: solid, liquid, gas.
- solids have a definite shape and volume
- liquids do not have a definite shape but have a definite volume
- gases do not hold their shape or volume

3.2b Temperature can affect the state of matter of a substance.

3.2c Changes in the properties or materials of objects can be observed and described.

Key Idea 4: Energy exists in many forms, and when these forms change energy is conserved.

Performance Indicator 4.1: Describe a variety of forms of energy (e.g., heat, chemical, light) and the changes that occur in objects when they interact with those forms of energy.

Major Understandings:

4.1a Energy exists in various forms: heat, electric, sound, chemical, mechanical, light.

4.1b Energy can be transferred from one place to another.

4.1c Some materials transfer energy better than others (heat and electricity).

4.1d Energy and matter interact: water is evaporated by the Sun's heat; a bulb is lighted by means of electrical current; a musical instrument is played to produce sound; dark colors may absorb light, light colors may reflect light.

4.1e Electricity travels in a closed circuit.

4.1f Heat can be released in many ways, for example, by burning, rubbing (friction), or combining one substance with another.

Science Content Standards

4.1g Interactions with forms of energy can be either helpful or harmful.

Performance Indicator 4.2: Observe the way one form of energy can be transferred into another form of energy present in common situations (e.g., mechanical to heat energy, mechanical to electrical energy, chemical to heat energy).

Major Understandings:

4.2a Everyday events involve one form of energy being changed to another.
- animals convert food to heat and motion
- the Sun's energy warms the air and water

4.2b Humans utilize interactions between matter and energy.
- chemical to electrical, light, and heat: battery and bulb
- electrical to sound (e.g., doorbell buzzer)
- mechanical to sound (e.g., musical instruments, clapping)
- light to electrical (e.g., solar-powered calculator)

Key Idea 5: Energy and matter interact through forces that result in changes in motion.

Performance Indicator 5.1: Describe the effects of common forces (pushes and pulls) of objects, such as those caused by gravity, magnetism, and mechanical forces.

Major Understandings:

5.1a The position of an object can be described by locating it relative to another object or the background (e.g., on top of, next to, over, under, etc.).

5.1b The position or direction of motion of an object can be changed by pushing or pulling.

5.1c The force of gravity pulls objects toward the center of Earth.

5.1d The amount of change in the motion of an object is affected by friction.

5.1e Magnetism is a force that may attract or repel certain materials.

5.1f Mechanical energy may cause change in motion through the application of force and through the use of simple machines such as pulleys, levers, and inclined planes.

Performance Indicator 5.2: Describe how forces can operate across distances.

Major Understandings:

5.2a The forces of gravity and magnetism can affect objects through gases, liquids, and solids.

5.2b The force of magnetism on objects decreases as distance increases.

STANDARD 4: The Living Environment

Key Idea 1: Living things are both similar to and different from each other and from nonliving things.

Performance Indicator 1.1: Describe the characteristics of and variations between living and nonliving things.

Major Understandings:

1.1a Animals need air, water, and food in order to live and thrive.

1.1b Plants require air, water, nutrients, and light in order to live and thrive.

1.1c Nonliving things do not live and thrive.

1.1d Nonliving things can be human-created or naturally occurring.

Performance Indicator 1.2: Describe the life processes common to all living things.

Major Understandings:

1.2a Living things grow, take in nutrients, breathe, reproduce, eliminate waste, and die.

Key Idea 2: Organisms inherit genetic information in a variety of ways that result in continuity structure and function between parents and offspring.

Performance Indicator 2.1: Recognize that traits of living things are both inherited and acquired or learned.

Major Understandings:

2.1a Some traits of living things have been inherited (e.g., color of flowers and number of limbs of animals).

2.1b Some characteristics result from an individual's interactions with the environment and cannot be inherited by the next generation (e.g., having scars; riding a bicycle).

Performance Indicator 2.2: Recognize that for humans and other living things there is genetic continuity between generations.

Major Understandings:

2.2a Plants and animals closely resemble their parents and other individuals in their species.

2.2b Plants and animals can transfer specific traits to their offspring when they reproduce.

Key Idea 3: Individual organisms and species change over time.

Performance Indicator 3.1: Describe how the structures of plants and animals complement the environment of the plant or animal.

Major Understandings:

3.1a Each animal has different structures that serve different functions in growth, survival, and reproduction.
- wings, legs, or fins enable some animals to seek shelter and escape predators

- the mouth, including teeth, jaws, and tongue, enables some animals to eat and drink
- eyes, nose, ears, tongue, and skin of some animals enable the animals to sense their surroundings
- claws, shells, spines, feathers, fur, scales, and color of body covering enable some animals to protect themselves from predators and other environmental conditions, or enable them to obtain food
- some animals have parts that are used to produce sounds and smells to help the animal meet its needs
- the characteristics of some animals change as seasonal conditions change (e.g., fur grows and is shed to help regulate body heat; body fat is a form of stored energy and it changes as the seasons change)

3.1b Each plant has different structures that serve different functions in growth, survival, and reproduction.
- roots help support the plant and take in water and nutrients
- leaves help plants utilize sunlight to make food for the plant
- stems, stalks, trunks, and other similar structures provide support for the plant
- some plants have flowers
- flowers are reproductive structures of plants that produce fruit which contains seeds
- seeds contain stored food that aids in germination and the growth of young plants

3.1c In order to survive in their environment, plants and animals must be adapted to that environment.
- seeds disperse by a plant's own mechanism and/or in a variety of ways that can include wind, water, and animals
- leaf, flower, stem, and root adaptations may include variations in size, shape, thickness, color, smell, and texture
- animal adaptations include coloration for warning or attraction, camouflage, defense mechanisms, movement, hibernation, and migration

Performance Indicator 3.2: Observe that differences within a species may give individuals an advantage in surviving and reproducing.

Major Understandings:

3.2a Individuals within a species may compete with each other for food, mates, space, water, and shelter in their environment.

3.2b All individuals have variations, and because of these variations, individuals of a species may have an advantage in surviving and reproducing.

Key Idea 4: The continuity of life is sustained through reproduction and development.

Performance Indicator 4.1: Describe the major stages in the life cycles of selected plants and animals.

Major Understandings:

4.1a Plants and animals have life cycles. These may include beginning of a life, development into an adult, reproduction as an adult, and eventually death.

4.1b Each kind of plant goes through its own stages of growth and development that may include seed, young plant, and mature plant.

4.1c The length of time from beginning of development to death of the plant is called its life span.

4.1d Life cycles of some plants include changes from seed to mature plant.

4.1e Each generation of animals goes through changes in form from young to adult. This completed sequence of changes in form is called a life cycle. Some insects change from egg to larva to pupa to adult.

4.1f Each kind of animal goes through its own stages of growth and development during its life span.

4.1g The length of time from an animal's birth to its death is called its life span. Life spans of different animals vary.

Performance Indicator 4.2: Describe evidence of growth, repair, and maintenance, such as nails, hair, and bone, and the healing of cuts and bruises.

Major Understandings:

4.2a Growth is the process by which plants and animals increase in size.

4.2b Food supplies the energy and materials necessary for growth and repair.

Key Idea 5: Organisms maintain a dynamic equilibrium that sustains life.

Performance Indicator 5.1: Describe basic life functions of common living specimens (e.g., guppies, mealworms, gerbils).

Major Understandings:

5.1a All living things grow, take in nutrients, breathe, reproduce, and eliminate waste.

5.1b An organism's external physical features can enable it to carry out life functions in its particular environment.

Science Content Standards

Performance Indicator 5.2: Describe some survival behaviors of common living specimens.

Major Understandings:

5.2a Plants respond to changes in their environment. For example, the leaves of some green plants change position as the direction of light changes; the parts of some plants undergo seasonal changes that enable the plant to grow; seeds germinate, and leaves form and grow.

5.2b Animals respond to change in their environment, (e.g., perspiration, heart rate, breathing rate, eye blinking, shivering, and salivating).

5.2c Senses can provide essential information (regarding danger, food, mates, etc.) to animals about their environment.

5.2d Some animals, including humans, move from place to place to meet their needs.

5.2e Particular animal characteristics are influenced by changing environmental conditions including: fat storage in winter, coat thickness in winter, camouflage, shedding of fur.

5.2f Some animal behaviors are influenced by environmental conditions. These behaviors may include: nest building, hibernating, hunting, migrating, and communicating.

5.2g The health, growth, and development of organisms are affected by environmental conditions such as the availability of food, air, water, space, shelter, heat, and sunlight.

Performance Indicator 5.3: Describe the factors that help promote good health and growth in humans.

Major Understandings:

5.3a Humans need a variety of healthy foods, exercise, and rest in order to grow and maintain good health.

5.3b Good health habits include hand washing and personal cleanliness; avoiding harmful substances (including alcohol, tobacco, illicit drugs); eating a balanced diet; engaging in regular exercise.

Key Idea 6: Plants and animals depend on each other and their physical environment.

Performance Indicator 6.1: Describe how plants and animals, including humans, depend upon each other and the nonliving environment.

Major Understandings:

6.1a Green plants are producers because they provide the basic food supply for themselves and animals.

6.1b All animals depend on plants. Some animals (predators) eat other animals (prey).

6.1c Animals that eat plants for food may in turn become food for other animals. This sequence is called a food chain.

6.1d Decomposers are living things that play a vital role in recycling nutrients.

6.1e An organism's pattern of behavior is related to the nature of that organism's environment, including the kinds and numbers of other organisms present, the availability of food and other resources, and the physical characteristics of the environment.

6.1f When the environment changes, some plants and animals survive and reproduce, and others die or move to new locations.

Performance Indicator 6.2: Describe the relationship of the Sun as an energy source for living and nonliving cycles.

Major Understandings:

6.2a Plants manufacture food by utilizing air, water, and energy from the Sun.

6.2b The Sun's energy is transferred on Earth from plants to animals through the food chain.

6.2c Heat energy from the Sun powers the water cycle (see Physical Science Key Idea 2).

Key Idea 7: Human decisions and activities have had a profound impact on the physical and living environments.

Performance Indicator 7.1: Identify ways in which humans have changed their environment and the effects of those changes.

Major Understandings:

7.1a Humans depend on their natural and constructed environments.

7.1b Over time humans have changed their environment by cultivating crops and raising animals, creating shelter, using energy, manufacturing goods, developing means of transportation, changing populations, and carrying out other activities.

7.1c Humans, as individuals or communities, change environments in ways that can be either helpful or harmful for themselves and other organisms.

Credits

Abbreviation key: MMH=Macmillan/McGraw-Hill

Cover Photography Credits: Front Cover: Natural Selection Stock Photography. Spine: Gerry Ellis/Digital Vision, Ltd/Getty Images. Back Cover: Gerry Ellis/Digital Vision, Ltd/Getty Images.

Map Credits: Mapping Specialists, Ltd.

Illustration Credits: All illustrations are by Macmillan/McGraw-Hill (MMH).

Photography Credits: iv (t)George Grall/National Geographic Image Collection, **iv** (tr)Ken Cavanaugh/MMH, **iv** (b)MMH, **iv** (br)Siede Preis/Photodisc Green/Getty Images; **ix** StockTrek/Getty Images; **vi** Skip Moody/Dembinsky Photo Associates; **vii** Annie Griffiths Belt/National Geographic Image Collection; **viii** Chris Mattison/NHPA; **xii** (t)Valerie Giles/Photo Researchers, Inc., **xii** (bl)MMH, (bc)Peter Anderson/DK Images, (br)Tom Bean/CORBIS; **xiii** (t)Studio Photogram/Alamy, (cl)Arco Images/Alamy, (cl)Colin Keates/Courtesy of the Natural History Museum, London/DK Images, (cl)Colin Keates/Courtesy of the Natural History Museum, London/DK Images, (cl)Ken Cavanaugh/MMH, (cl)Visuals Unlimited/Getty Images, (b)Weatherstock/Peter Arnold, Inc.; **xiv** C Squared Studios/Getty Images; **1** Don Paulson Photography/SuperStock; **3** (t,tr,c,cr,b,br)MMH, (b)Siede Preis/Photodisc/Getty Images; **4** (b)Hans Schouten/Foto Natura/Minden Pictures, (bl)Brand X Pictures/Punchstock, (br)Michael Orton/Getty Images; **5** (cl)Martin Ruegner/Getty Images, (cr)Marie Read/Animals Animals/Earth Scenes; **6** (cl)Ken Cavanaugh/MMH, (cl)Klaus Uhlenhut/Animals Animals/Earth Scenes, (cr)Brand X Pictures/Punchstock, (b)George Grall/National Geographic Image Collection, (br)Siede Preis/Photodisc/Getty Images; **7** (cl)Siede Preis/Getty Images, (cr,bl)Photodisc/Getty Images, (b)Norbert Rosing/National Geographic Image Collection; **8** (cl)David Boag/PictureQuest, (c)Hans Pfletschinger/Peter Arnold, Inc., (cr)Kim Taylor/Bruce Coleman Inc., (b)Michael Durham/Minden Pictures; **10–11** Bob Elsdale/Getty Images; **11** (t)D. Parer & E. Parer-Cook/Auscape/Minden Pictures, (t)Photodisc/Getty Images, (c)Jeff Foott/Getty Images, (b)Stephen Dalton/Minden Pictures; **12** (b)Dan Suzio/Photo Researchers, Inc., (br)Geoff Brightling/DK Images, (br)Ken Karp/MMH; **13** James Balog/Getty Images; **15** (t)Photodisc/Getty Images, (b)Geoff Brightling/DK Images, (br)Dan Suzio/Photo Researchers, Inc.; **16** (t, bl)C Squared Studios/Getty Images, (bc)Photodisc Green/Getty Images, (br)Brand X Pictures/Alamy; **17** Elizabeth Ballengee/MazerStock; **19** Daniel Cox/Jupiterimages; **20** (cr)Courtesy of American Maple Museum, (b)Elizabeth Knox/Masterfile, (bkgd)Robert Estall/CORBIS; **21** Nature Picture Library/Alamy; **22** (c)WCS/J. Maher/Bronx Zoo, (bkgd)Diane Shapiro/Peter Arnold, Inc.; **23** Rod Planck/Photo Researchers, Inc.; **24** Frank Krahmer/Masterfile; **25** (c)Papilio/Alamy, (b)Tom Bean/CORBIS; **26** Peter Finger/CORBIS; **27** MMH; **28** (t)Meul/ARCO/naturepl.com, (b)John Cancalosi/Peter Arnold, Inc.; **29** (c)Papilio/Alamy, (r)du Sud/Photolibrary.com, (b)Royalty-Free/CORBIS, (l)Steve Taylor/SPL/Photo Researchers, Inc.; **30** Burke/Getty Images; **31** (t)Jim Allan/Alamy, (t)Royalty-Free/CORBIS, (b)Siede Preis/Getty Images; **34–35** Neil Fletcher/DK Images; **35** MMH; **36** Claudius Thiriet/Grandeur Nature/Hoa-Qui/Imagestate; **37** (t)Ingram Publishing/age fotostock, (t)Karen Tweedy-Holmes/CORBIS, (b)Malcolm Case-Green/Alamy; **38** (l)Blickwinkel/Alamy, (cl)David Sieren/Visuals Unlimited, (cr)Peter Gardner/DK Images, (r)Derek Hall/DK Images; **39** (t)Jane Grushow/Grant Heilman Photography, Ken Cavanaugh/MMH; **40** (tc)Nuno Tavares, (tr)Peter Anderson/DK Images, (tr)britishcolumbiaphotos.com/Alamy, (c)Doug Sokell/Visuals Unlimited, (bl)Tom Bean/CORBIS, (br)David R. Frazier Photolibrary, Inc./Alamy; **41** (l)John Henwood/Alamy, (t)C.W. Biedel, (cl)Peter Arnold Inc./Alamy; **42** Imagestate/Alamy; **43** (l)Herbert Kehrer/zefa/CORBIS, (cr)DIOMEDIA/Alamy, (r)PhotoAlto/Punchstock, **44** Tim Laman/Getty Images; **45** MMH; **46** (l)Siede Preis/Getty Images, (t)Brand X Pictures/Punchstock, (r)Papilio/Alamy, (b)Gary Crabbe; **47** (t)Brand X Pictures/Punchstock, (b)Russell Illig/Getty Images; **48** (l)David Noton/Getty Images, (r)Dave G. Houser/CORBIS; **49** Fabrice Bettex/Alamy; **51** (tl)Edward Parker/Alamy, (r)Dominique Halleux/Peter Arnold, Inc.; **52** (b)Peter Fakler/Alamy, (bkgd)Arco Images/Alamy, (bkgd)James Strawser/Grant Heilman Photography; **53** Nico Tondini/age fotostock; **54** Wilson Goodrich/Index Stock Imagery; **55** (b)Jerome Wexler/Visuals Unlimited, (bkgd)Nancy Sheehan/PhotoEdit; **57** (tl,tr)Pdphoto.org, (b)George H. H. Huey/CORBIS; **58–59** Dwight Kuhn Photography; **59** (t)franzfoto.com/Alamy, (c)Burke/Getty Images, (b)Juergen & Christine Sohns/Animals Animals/Earth Scenes, (bl)John P. Marechal/Bruce Coleman Inc.; **60–61** Tui De Roy/Minden Pictures; **61** (t)Kevin Schafer/zefa/CORBIS, (cl)Fritz Rauschenbach/zefa/CORBIS, (cl)Werner H. Mueller/zefa/CORBIS, (c)Michael & Patricia Fogden/CORBIS, (b)Gary Bell/oceanwideimages.com, (bc)David A. Northcott/CORBIS; **62** franzfoto.com/Alamy; **63** (t)Danita Delimont/Alamy, (tl)Herve Berthoule/Jacana/Photo Researchers, Inc., (cr)Bruce Coleman, Inc./Alamy, (b)Wendell Metzen/Bruce Coleman Inc.; **64** (cl)Xavier Desmier/Rapho/Imagestate, (cr)Royalty-Free/CORBIS; **65** (t)Bob Elsdale/Getty Images, (c)E. R. Degginger/Animals Animals/Earth Scenes, (b)Tim Ridley/Getty Images; **68–69** Brand X Pictures/Punchstock; **69** Nancy Ney/Digital Vision/Getty Images; **70** (cl,bc,br)Jane Burton/DK Images, (c)Garrison Ron/CORBIS Sygma, (cr)Reuters/CORBIS, (bl)DK Images; **71** Daniel A. Bedell/Animals Animals/Earth Scenes; **72** (tl)Papilio/Alamy, (tc)John P. Marechal/Bruce Coleman Inc., (tr)John T. Fowler/Alamy; **73** (t)Phototake/Alamy, (tl)DIOMEDIA/Alamy; **74** (b)Courtesy of Nancy Simmons, (t)Sundell Larsen/Photodisc/Getty Images; **75** (t)Jane Burton/Bruce Coleman Inc., (b)Wildlife Pictures/Peter Arnold, Inc.; **76–77** Chris Mattison/NHPA; **77** MMH; **78** (l)Comstock/Punchstock, (cr)Michael Dick/Animals Animals/Earth Scenes, (b)Juergen & Christine Sohns/Animals Animals/Earth Scenes; **79** (t)Richard Moran/AlaskaStock.com, (t)Steve Maslowski/Visuals Unlimited, (tr)David Fritts/Animals Animals/Earth Scenes, (b)David A. Northcott/CORBIS; **80** (t)Arthur Morris/CORBIS, (tl)Dietmar Nill/Foto Natura/Minden Pictures, (b)Georgette Douwma/Getty Images; **81** (t)Creatas/Punchstock, (c)Hemera/age fotostock, (b)PhotoDisc/Getty Images; **82** (cl)David Shale/naturepl.com, (cr)Steve Bloom Images/Alamy; **83** Jane Burton/DK Images; **84–85** Richard Du Toit/naturepl.com; **85** Royalty-Free/CORBIS; **86** Anup Shah/Getty Images; **86–87** John Conrad/CORBIS; **88** John P. Marechal/Bruce Coleman Inc.; **89** (tl)Arthur Morris/CORBIS, (tr)Royalty-Free/CORBIS, (cr)Photodisc/Getty Images; **90–91** Victoria McCormick/Animals Animals/Earth Scenes; **91** (t)Annie Griffiths Belt/National Geographic Image Collection, (cl)Christopher Ratier/Photo Researchers, Inc., (c)Thinkstock/Jupiterimages, (b)Ken Lucas/Visuals Unlimited; **92–93** Georgette Douwma/Getty Images; **93** (t,c)MMH, (br)Stephen Krasemen/NHPA; **94** (c)Annie Griffiths Belt/National Geographic Image Collection, (b)Michael Quinton/Minden Pictures; **94–95** Klein/Peter Arnold, Inc.; **95** Karl Switakx/NHPA; **97** DK Limited/CORBIS; **98** (b)Papilio/Alamy, (t,cr,cl,b)Robert Pickett/Alamy, (c)Nigel Cattlin/Alamy; **99** (t)age fotostock/SuperStock, (c)Donald Specker/Animals Animals, (c)Gary W. Carter/CORBIS, (b)Thomas & Pat Leeson/Photo Researchers; **100–101** Christophe Ratier/Photo Researchers, Inc.; **101** (t,c,tc)MMH, (b)Guenter Rossenbach/zefa/CORBIS, (bc)Gary Meszaros/Visuals Unlimited, (br)Arthur Morris/CORBIS; **105** Tom Vezo/Minden Pictures; **107** (t)George Grall/Getty Images, (tr)Frank Greenaway/DK Images, (cl)Creatas/Punchstock, (cr)Dynamic Graphics Group/IT Stock Free/Alamy, (cr)Dynamic Graphics Group/IT Stock Free/Alamy, (b)Frank Greenaway/DK Images; **108–109** Bob Krist/CORBIS; **109** MMH; **110** Thinkstock/Jupiterimages; **110–111** David Hosking/Photo Researchers, Inc.; **111** (t)Jim Zuckerman/CORBIS, (b)Catherine Ledner/Getty Images; **112** (cl)Schafer & Hill/Getty Images, (cr)Arthur Morris/Visuals Unlimited; **113** Fred Bavendam/Minden Pictures; **114** (c)Ken Lucas/Visuals Unlimited, (b)James L. Amos/National Geographic Image Collection; **115** Jonathan Blair/CORBIS;

116 Dennis Finnin/American Museum of Natural History;
116–117 Royalty-Free/CORBIS; 117 Courtesy American Museum
of Natural History; 118 (c)C Squared Studios/Getty Images,
(b)Photodisc/Getty Images; 119 (c)C Squared Studios/Getty
Images, (cr)Royalty-Free/CORBIS; 120 Jane Burton/DK Images;
121 (c)PhotoDisc/Getty Images, (b)Jane Burton/DK Images;
123 (cl)Royalty-Free/CORBIS, (cr)ThinkStock/Jupiterimages;
124 Tom Vezo/Minden Pictures; 128 (b)Jim Reed/Photo
Researchers, Inc., (bkgd)OAA Photo Library; 130 (c)Anne
Ackermann/Getty Images, (bkgd)Mark Dyball/Alamy; 131 Food Pix/
Jupiter Images; 132–133 Royalty-Free/CORBIS; 133 (t)Photomaster/
MMH, (tl)Steve Satushek/Getty Images, (c)Robert Glusic/Getty
Images, (b)Warren Faidley/Weatherstock; 134–135 Steve Satushek/
Getty Images; 135 (t,c)MMH, (b)Stockbyte/Getty Images;
136 (bl,bc)MMH, (bl)Stockbyte/Getty Images, (br)Stuart Pearce/
Pixtal/age fotostock; 137 (t)Layne Kennedy/CORBIS, (c)Galen
Rowell/CORBIS, (bl)Steve Satushek/Getty Images, (bc)Tony
Freeman/PhotoEdit; 138 (cl)Andrew Holt/Alamy, (b)Steven Puetzer/
Masterfile; 139 (t)Tony Freeman/PhotoEdit, (b)Markus Dlouhy/Peter
Arnold, Inc.; 140 Rudi Von Briel/PhotoEdit; 141 (t)Dennis
MacDonald/PhotoEdit, (tr)MMH; 142–143 Frans Lemmens/Getty
Images; 143 MMH; 144 Royalty-Free/CORBIS; 145 (t)David
Middleton/Photo Researchers, Inc., (t)George McCarthy/naturepl.
com, (tl)Digital Archive Japan/Alamy, (tr)Guenter Rossenbach/
zefa/CORBIS; 146–147 Alan Kearney/Getty Images; 148 (t)Image
Farm, Inc., (inset)Robert Brenner/Photo Edit; 149 (l)Robert Warren/
Getty Images, Inc., (tr)MMH, (br)Siede Preis/Getty Images;
150–151 Richard Wong/Alamy; 152 Robert Glusic/Photodisc/Getty
Images; 153 (t)Gerald & Buff Corsi/Visuals Unlimited, (b)Warren
Faidley/Weatherstock; 154 (cl)Courtesy of USDA Natural Resources
Conservation Service, (cl)Tina Manley/Alamy, (b)Stockbyte/
Punchstock, (bl)Royalty-Free/CORBIS, (bl)Steven Puetzer/
Masterfile; 155 (t)Jim Reed/Getty Images, (b)Comstock/Punchstock;
156 (t)Peter Menzel/SPL/Photo Researchers, Inc., (b)Kent Wood/
Photo Researchers, Inc.; 157 (c)NOAA/AP Images, (cr)David R.
Frazier/Photo Researchers, Inc.; 158 Gallo Images/CORBIS;
158–159 Macduff Everton/CORBIS; 160–161 Bertram G. Murray/
Animals Animals/Earth Scenes; 161 imagebroker/Alamy;
162 (bl)Mimotito/Digital Vision/Getty Images, (br)Andre Jenny/
Alamy; 163 (t)PhotoLink/Getty Images, (c)Adrian Sherratt/Alamy;
164–165 Brand X Pictures/Punchstock; 165 (cl)Shigemi Numazawa/
Atlas Photo Bank/Photo Researchers, Inc., (b)Brand X Pictures/
Punchstock; 166–167 Walter Bibikow Index Stock Imagery; 167 MMH;
171 Jon Hicks/CORBIS; 172 Jeff Greenberg/PhotoEdit; 173 (t)Ken
Karp/MMH, (b)PhotoLink/Getty Images; 174–175 Andre Jenny/
Alamy; 175 Ken Karp/MMH; 176 (bl)Bill Frymire/Masterfile,
(br)Richard Hutchings/PhotoEdit; 177 (b)Stockdisc/Punchstock,
(bl)Photodisc/Getty Images, (br)Tony Anderson/Getty Images;
180 (tl)Royalty-Free/CORBIS, (tr)Shoot Pty. Ltd./Index Stock
Imagery; 182–183 Bill Brooks/Masterfile; 183 MMH; 185 (t)NASA/
Photo Researchers, Inc.; 186 (t)Stockbyte/Punchstock;
186–187 Larry Landolfi/Photo Researchers, Inc.; 188 Gerard
Lodriguss/Photo Researchers, Inc.; 189 Picto's/Jupiterimages;
190 MMH; 191 (t)Stockbyte/Punchstock, (b)Shigemi Numazawa/
Atlas Photo Bank/Photo Researchers, Inc.; 192 Robert Spoenlein/
zefa/CORBIS; 193 Werner H.Mueller/zefa/CORBIS; 194–195 Stock
Connection/Alamy; 196 (b)Brand X Pictures/Punchstock, (bl)Picto's/
Jupiterimages; 197 (t)Gordon & Cathy Illg/Animals Animals/Earth
Scenes, (b)Stockbyte/Punchstock; 202 (t)Jim Schwabel/Grant
Heilman Photography, Inc., (b)Bettmann/CORBIS, (bkgd)Joseph
Sohm; (c)Visions of America/CORBIS; 203 John Sommers II/
Reuters/CORBIS; 204 (t) Henryk Kaiser/Alamy, SuperStock, Inc./
SuperStock; 205 Masterfile Royalty-Free Div.; 206–207 Andre
Jenny/Alamy; 207 (t,b)Ken Karp/MMH, (cl)Michel Tcherevkoff/
Getty Images, (c)C Squared Studios/Getty Images; 208–209 Paul
Chesley/Getty Images; 210 Ariel Skelley/CORBIS; 211 Ken Karp/
MMH; 212 (cl)Kevin Schafer/zefa/CORBIS, (cr)Ken Cavanaugh/MMH;

213 Ken Karp/MMH; 214 Comstock/PictureQuest; 216–217 Ken
Karp/MMH; 217 MMH; 218 (bc)Ken Karp/MMH, (br)Nikreates/
Alamy; 219 Ken Karp/MMH; 220 (t)Brand X Pictures/PictureQuest,
(tr)Photodisc/Getty Images, (b)MMH; 221 Ken Karp/MMH; 222 (t)C
Squared Studios/Getty Images, (c)Gary Braasch/CORBIS, (b)C
Squared Studios/Getty Images, (bkgd)Ryan McVay/CORBIS;
223 (t)V&A Images/Alamy, (c)Louie Psihoyos/Getty Images, (b)CSA
Plastock/Getty Images, (bkgd)Royalty-Free/CORBIS; 224–225 Ken
Karp/MMH; 225 MMH; 226 (t)Michel Tcherevkoff/Getty Images,
(b)Mark Viker/Getty Images, (bl)Digital Vision/Punchstock; 227 Ken
Karp/MMH; 228 (l)Buzz Pictures/Alamy, (b)Ken Karp/MMH,
(br)Heka agence photo/Alamy; 229 (t)Keate/Masterfile, (tl,tr)Ken
Karp/MMH, (tr)Stock Food/SuperStock; 230 Sharon L. Jonz/Photis/
PictureQuest; 231–233 Ken Karp/MMH; 233 MMH; 234 (cl,c,b)Ken
Karp/MMH, (cl)Royalty-Free/CORBIS; 235 (t)David M. Dennis/
Animals Animals/Earth Scenes, (bl)imagebroker/Alamy, (br)Mike
McClure/Index Stock Imagery; 236 (t)Steve Schott/DK Images,
(cl,c)Siede Preis/Getty Images, (c)Bryan Mullennix/Getty Images,
(b)Steve Gorton/DK Images; 237 (tl)Photodisc/Getty Images,
(tc)F. Schussler/Getty Images; 238 MMH; 239 Brand X Pictures/
PictureQuest, Jacques Cornell for MMH, Ken Cavanagh for MMH;
240–241 Douglas Peebles Photography/Alamy; 241 MMH;
242 (t)John A. Rizzo/Getty Images, (b)Charles O'Rear/CORBIS,
(bl)PhotoDisc/Getty Images; 244 (t)Nora Good/Masterfile, (b)Arno
Gasteiger/Stock Central/age fotostock; 245 Ken Karp/MMH;
246 (tl)William Thomas Cain/Getty Images, (t)Binney & Smith,
(b)Stockdisc/Punchstock; 247 (tl)Steve Rasmussen/AP Images,
(tr)William Thomas Cain/Getty Images, (b)Dave Mager/Index
Stock Imagery, (bl)Stockdisc/Punchstock; 248 (t)Stockdisc/
Punchstock, (b)Ken Karp/MMH; 249 D. Hurst/Alamy; 250 Brooke
Slezak/Getty Images; 251 Deborah Jaffe/Photodisc/Getty Images;
253 (tl)imagebroker/Alamy, (tr)Dorling Kindersley/Getty Images,
(b)C Squared Studios/Getty Images; 254–255 Jean Brooks/Getty
Images; 255 (t)Daniel Dempster/Bruce Coleman Inc., (cl)Richard
Hutchings/PhotoEdit, (c,b)Michael Scott/MMH; 256–257 Adam
Alberti/911 Pictures; 257 Mark Raycroft/Minden Pictures; 258 (l)Pat
Doyle/CORBIS, (cl,b,bl,bc)C Squared Studios/Getty Images,
(cl)Royalty-Free/CORBIS, (r)Hugh Threlfall/Alamy, (bl)Brand X
Pictures/Punchstock, (b)Stockbyte/PictureQuest, (b)Pat Doyle/
CORBIS; 259 (t)Tim Davis/Getty Images, (c)Daniel Dempster/Bruce
Coleman Inc., (b)Ian & Karen Stewart/Bruce Coleman Inc.,
(br)Dennis Novak/Getty Images; 260 (t)G.K. & Vikki Hart/Getty
Images, (b)Michael Scott/MMH; 260–261 Gerard Lacz/Animals
Animals/Earth Scenes; 261 (t)Andy Rouse/Getty Images, (t)Anup
Shah/Photodisc/Getty Images, (t)Tracey Rich/naturepl.com;
262 Bob Daemmrich/Photo Edit; 263 Ken Karp/MMH, Michael
Scott/MMH; 264–265 David Madison/Getty Images; 265 MMH;
266 (t)Photodisc/Getty Images, (b)Thomas Barwick/Photodisc/
Getty Images; 266–267 Creatas/Punchstock; 267 (t)Norbert
Schaefer/CORBIS, (t)Photodisc/Getty Images, (b)Rolf Bruderer/
CORBIS; 268 (b)Dan Burn-Forti /Getty Images; 268–269 Creatas/
Punchstock; 269 (t)David Young-Wolff/PhotoEdit, (c)Richard
Hutchings/PhotoEdit, (b)Photodisc/Getty Images; 270 (t)Robert
W. Ginn/PhotoEdit, (b)Peter Arnold, Inc./Alamy; 271 Scott T. Baxter/
Getty Images; 272 Denis Finnin/American Museum of Natural
History; 272–273 Roger Ressmeyer/CORBIS; 273 Jean-Charles
Cuillandre/CFHT/Photo Researchers, Inc.; 274–275 Romy Ragan/
Pixtal/age fotostock; 275 MMH; 277 Steve Cole/Photodisc/Getty
Images; 278 Kim Karpeles/Alamy;279 (t)DK Images, (c)C Squared
Studios/Getty Images, (c)Image Source/Punchstock; 280 Doug
Allen/naturepl.com; 283 MMH; 284 (l,c)Ken Karp/MMH, (b)Charles
Bowman/Alamy; 285 (t)Comstock Images/Alamy, (c,cr,b)MMH,
(bl)PhotoLink/Getty Images; 286 (t,tc)Michael Scott/MMH,
(c)photolibrary.com pty. ltd./Index Stock Imagery; 287 (t)Planetary
Visions Ltd/Photo Researchers, Inc.; (c)Ingram Publishing/Alamy;
288 Ken Karp/MMH; 294 (c)David Young-Wolff/PhotoEdit, (b)Ken
Karp/MMH; 295 (t)Ken Karp/MMH, (b)First Light/CORBIS;

Credits

296–297 Kelly-Mooney Photography/CORBIS; **297** (t)Jim West/
Alamy, (tl)Comstock/Punchstock; **298–299** Designpics/Inmagine
Corporation LLC; **299** Ken Karp/MMH; **300** Darryl Leniuk/Masterfile;
301 (t)Jim West/Alamy, (c)David Young-Wolff/PhotoEdit, (b)Royalty
Free/CORBIS; **302** (b)Chad Ehlers/Alamy, (bl)Marvin E. Newman/
Getty Images, (bc,br)Ken Karp/MMH; **303** (t)Ken Karp/MMH,
(c)Stock Connection Distribution/Alamy; **304** (t)Ken Karp/MMH,
(c)Photodisc/Punchstock, (b)Swerve/Alamy; **305** Ken Karp/MMH;
306–307 Gideon Mendel/CORBIS; **307** MMH; **308** (t)Image Source/
Alamy, (b)Comstock/Punchstock; **309** (t)C Squared Studios/Getty
Images, (b)Comstock/Punchstock; **310** (t)Yann Arthus-Bertrand/
CORBIS, (b)PCL/Alamy; **311** C Squared Studios/Getty Images;
312 image100/Punchstock; **313** (t)Philip Rostron/Masterfile,
(b)C Squared Studios/Getty Images; **314** (t)Gary W. Carter/CORBIS,
(tl)Robert Slade/Alamy, (cl)Robert W. Ginn/PhotoEdit, (cr)Craig
Orsini/Index Stock Imagery; **316–317** Sanford/Agliolo/CORBIS;
317 MMH; **318–319** Ken Karp/MMH; **320** (c)ThinkStock LLC/Index
Stock Imagery, (b)Lee Cohen/CORBIS; **321** (t)Chris Collins/CORBIS,
(b)Comstock/Punchstock; **322–323** Ken Karp/MMH; **324–325** Larry
Fisher/Masterfile; **325–326** MMH; **328** Carson Ganci/PictureQuest;
329 Roger Ressmeyer/CORBIS; **331** Nicholas Veasey/Getty Images;
332 Creatas Images/Punchstock; **333** Gavriel Jecan/CORBIS;
334 Image Source/Punchstock; **335** Ken Karp/MMH; **337** (r)Ken
Karp/MMH, (bl)ThinkStock LLC/Index Stock Imagery; **R1** (t)MMH,
(b)Jules Frazier/Getty Images; **R3–R5** MMH; **R6** (t)Ryan McVay/
Getty Images, (bl)Photodisc/Getty Images, (br)MMH; **R7** Jules
Frazier/Getty Images; **R8** Imagestate/Punchstock; **R9–R11** MMH;
R13 (t)David Loftus/Getty Images, (cl,b)C Squared Studios/Getty
Images; **R14** (cl)Purestock/Punchstock, (cr)Photodisc Collection/
Getty Images; **R15** Stockdisc/Punchstock; **R16** Richard Hutchings/
PhotoEdit; **R17** (tl)Jack Hollingsworth/Getty Images, (tr)David
Buffington/Getty Images, (cl)Photodisc/Punchstock, (cr)D. Berry/
PhotoLink/Getty Images; **R18** (cl)PhotoLink/Getty Images, (c)MMH,
(c)Photo by Master Sgt. Michael A. Kaplan/U.S. Air Force,
(b)Richard Chung/Reuters/CORBIS, (br)StockTrek/Getty Images;
R19 (t)GK & Vikki Hart/Getty Images, (t)Juergen & Christine Sohns/
Animals Animals/Earth Scenes, (tr)Bruce Coleman, Inc./Alamy,
(c)Tony Freeman/PhotoEdit, (cr)Ken Karp/MMH, (b)David A.
Northcott/CORBIS; **R20** (t)F. Schussler/PhotoLink/Getty Images,
(t)Photodisc/Getty Images, (c)Gerald & Buff Corsi/Visuals
Unlimited, (c)Nora Good/Masterfile; **R21** (t)Thinkstock/
Jupiterimages, (tr)Schafer & Hill/Getty Images, (c)Jonathan Blair/
CORBIS, (cr)Royalty-Free/CORBIS; **R22** (tr)Creatas/Punchstock,
(tr)Photodisc/Getty Images, (tr)Thomas Barwick/Photodisc/Getty
Images, (c)Ken Lucas/Visuals Unlimited, (cr)Richard Hutchings/
PhotoEdit, (b)Ken Karp/MMH, (br)Jim West/Alamy; **R23** (t)Ken
Karp/MMH, (tr)Photodisc/Getty Images, (c)Darryl Leniuk/Masterfile,
(cr)Annie Griffiths Belt/National Geographic Image Collection,
(b)John P. Marechal/Bruce Coleman Inc., (br)Burke/Triolo
Productions/Brand X Pictures/Getty Images; **R24** (t)Michael Scott/
MMH, (tr)DK Images, (tr)Jane Burton/DK Images, (cr)Mark Viker/
Getty Images, (cr)Sanford/Agliolo/CORBIS, (b)Ken Karp/MMH,
(br)franzfoto.com/Alamy; **R25** (t)Ariel Skelley/CORBIS, (cr)Daniel
Dempster/Bruce Coleman Inc., (b)Shigemi Numazawa/Atlas Photo
Bank/Photo Researchers, Inc., (br)Royalty Free/CORBIS; **R26** (t)Ken
Karp/MMH, (tr,br)C Squared Studios/Getty Images, (c)Planetary
Visions Ltd./Photo Researchers, Inc., (b)Steve Satushek/Getty
Images, (br)Royalty-Free/CORBIS; **R27** (t)Christopher Ratier/Photo
Researchers, Inc., (tr)Tom Vezo/Minden Pictures, (c)John T. Fowler/
Alamy, (cr)Ken Cavanaugh/MMH, (b)Ken Karp/MMH, (br)Steve
Cole/Photodisc/Getty Images; **R28** (t)Michael Scott/MMH,
(tr)Wendell Metzen/Bruce Coleman Inc., (c)Papilio/Alamy,
(b)Steve Cole/Photodisc/Getty Images, (br)Tom Bean/CORBIS;
R29 (t)Jonathan Nourok/PhotoEdit, (tr)Image Source/Alamy,
(c)Andy Rouse/Getty Images, (cr)Brand X Pictures/Punchstock,
(b)Warren Faidley/Weatherstock, (br)Roger Ressmeyer/CORBIS;
R30 (t,b)Ken Karp/MMH, (t)MMH, (tr)Brand X Pictures/Punchstock,
(c)Comstock/Punchstock.